WITH NOTES AND TAB

# THE BEST OF Queen FOR GUITAR

## CONTENTS

ISBN 978-0-7935-3848-5

7777 W. Bluemound Rd. P.O. Box 13819 Milwaukee, WI 53213

# BICYCLE RACE

Words and Music by FREDDIE MERCURY

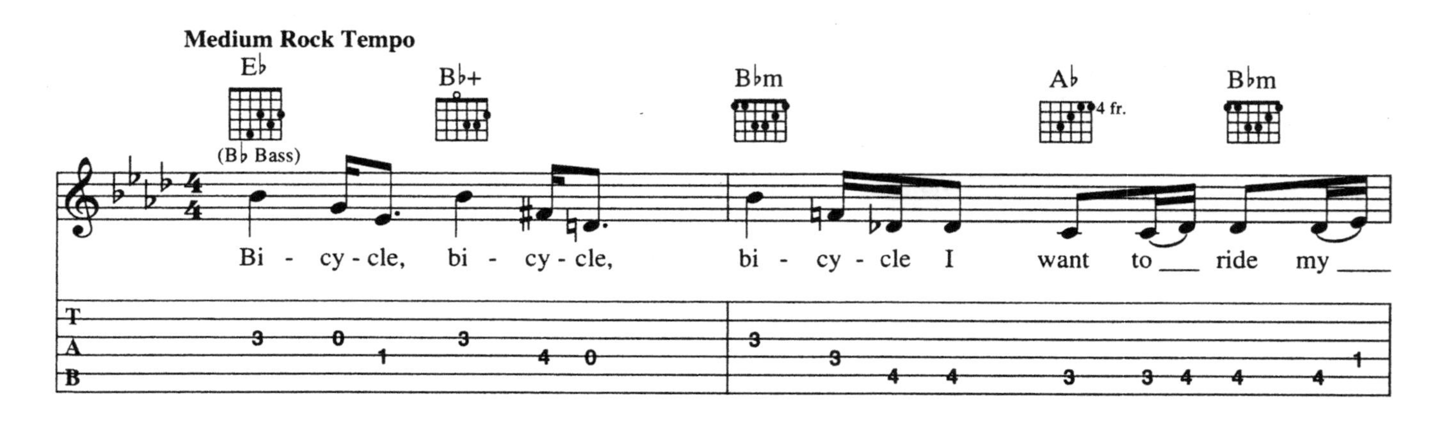


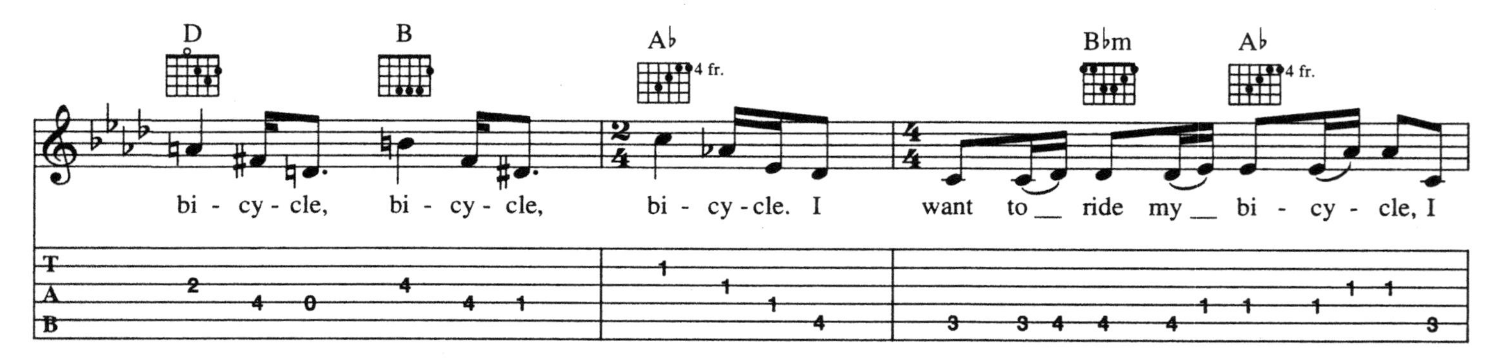

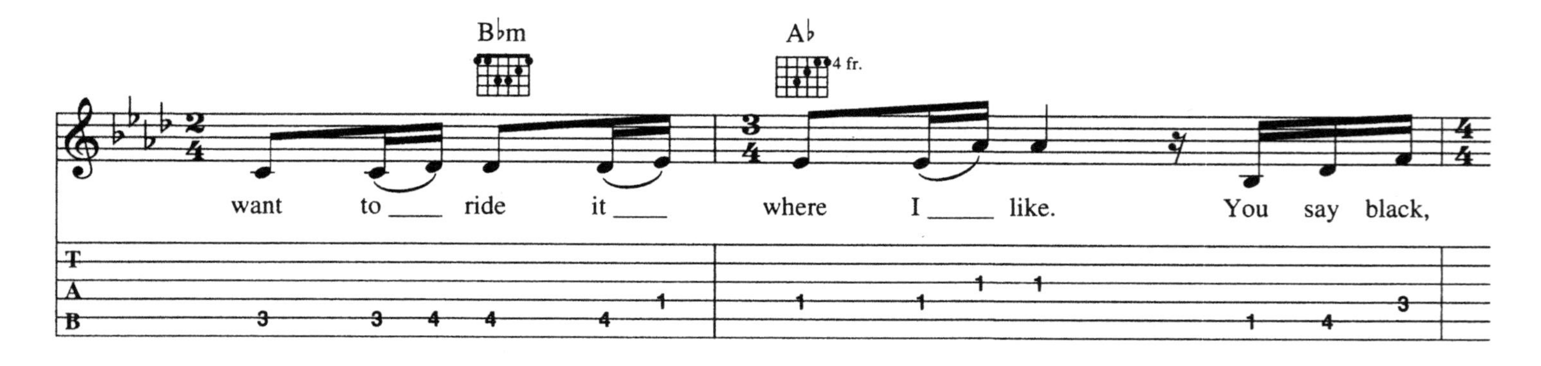

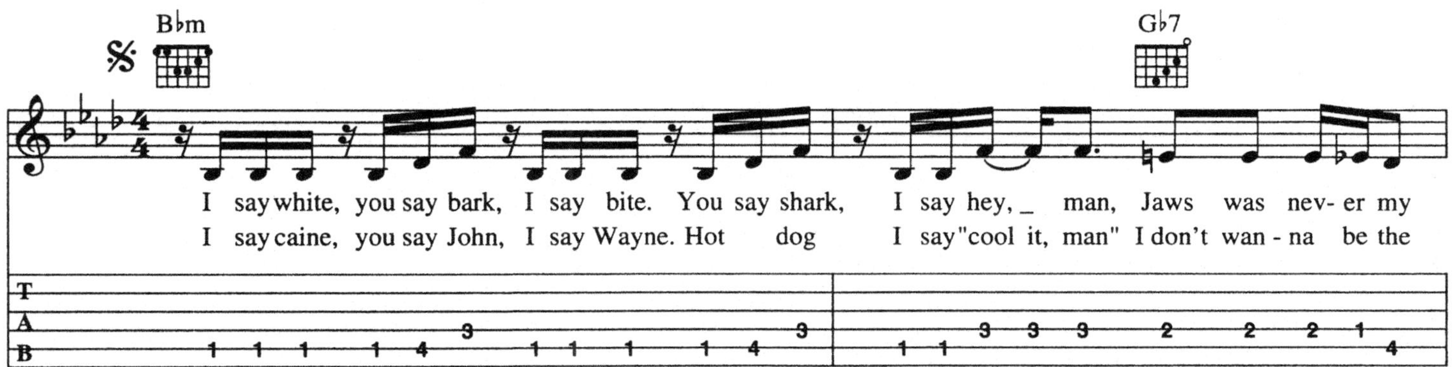
B♭m
G♭7
I say white, you say bark, I say bite. You say shark, I say hey, _ man, Jaws was nev- er my
I say caine, you say John, I say Wayne. Hot dog I say "cool it, man" I don't wan - na be the

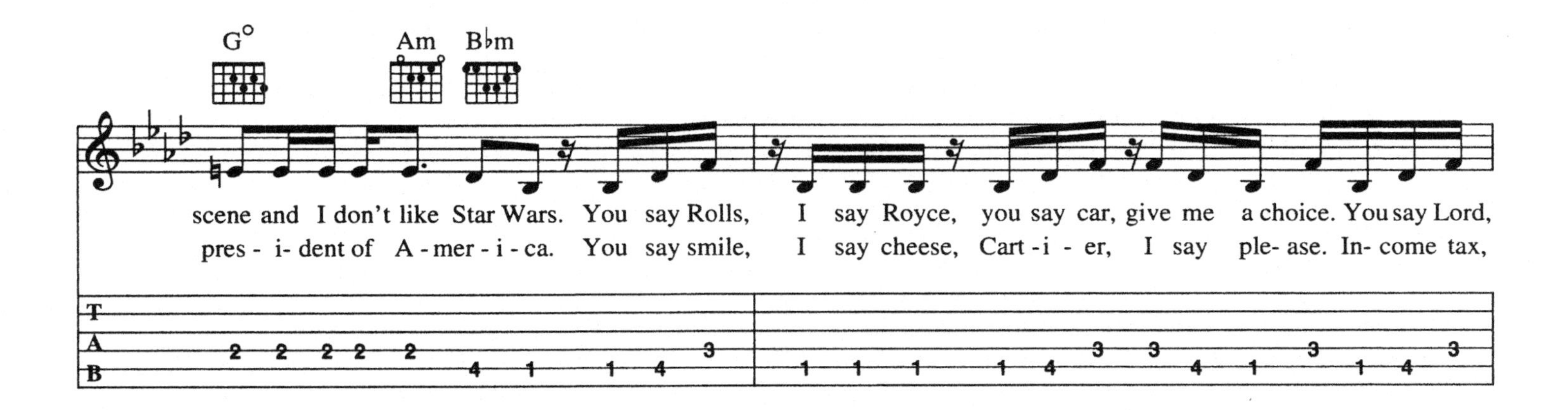
G°
Am
B♭m
scene and I don't like Star Wars. You say Rolls, I say Royce, you say car, give me a choice. You say Lord,
pres - i- dent of A - mer - i - ca. You say smile, I say cheese, Cart - i - er, I say ple- ase. In- come tax,

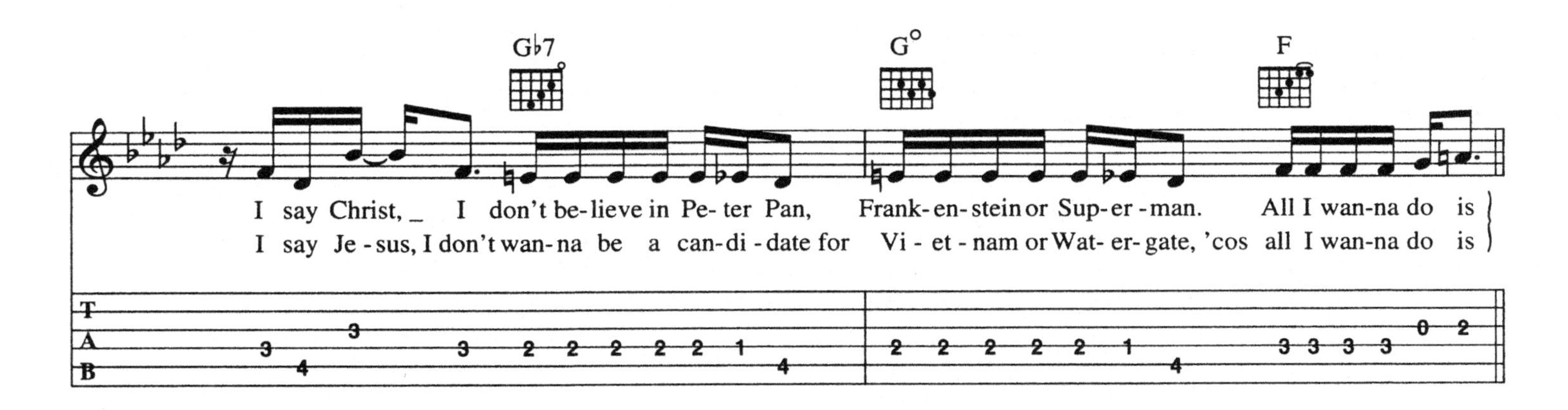
G♭7
G°
F
I say Christ, _ I don't be- lieve in Pe- ter Pan, Frank- en- stein or Sup- er - man. All I wan- na do is
I say Je - sus, I don't wan- na be a can- di - date for Vi - et - nam or Wat- er- gate, 'cos all I wan-na do is

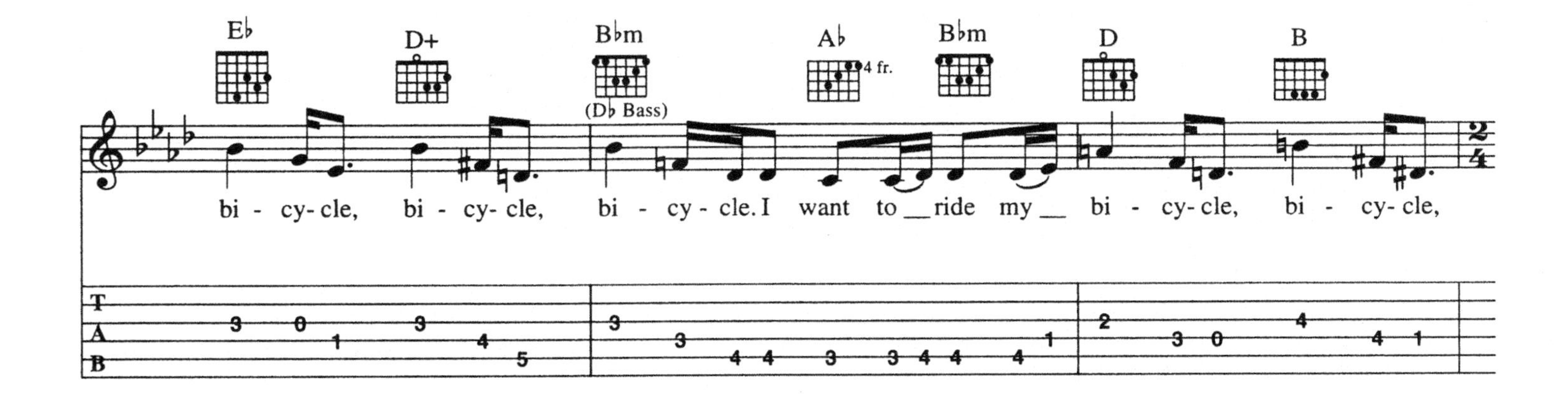
E♭
D+
B♭m
(D♭ Bass)
A♭
4 fr.
B♭m
D
B
bi - cy- cle, bi - cy- cle, bi - cy - cle. I want to _ ride my _ bi - cy- cle, bi - cy- cle,

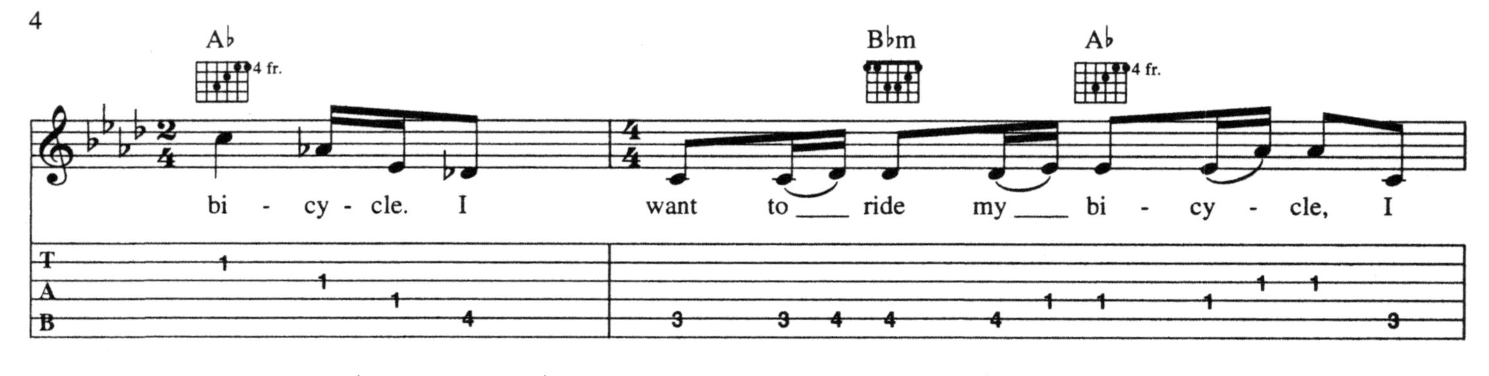
A♭
4 fr.
B♭m
A♭
4 fr.
bi - cy - cle. I
want to ___ ride my ___ bi - cy - cle, I
T
A
B

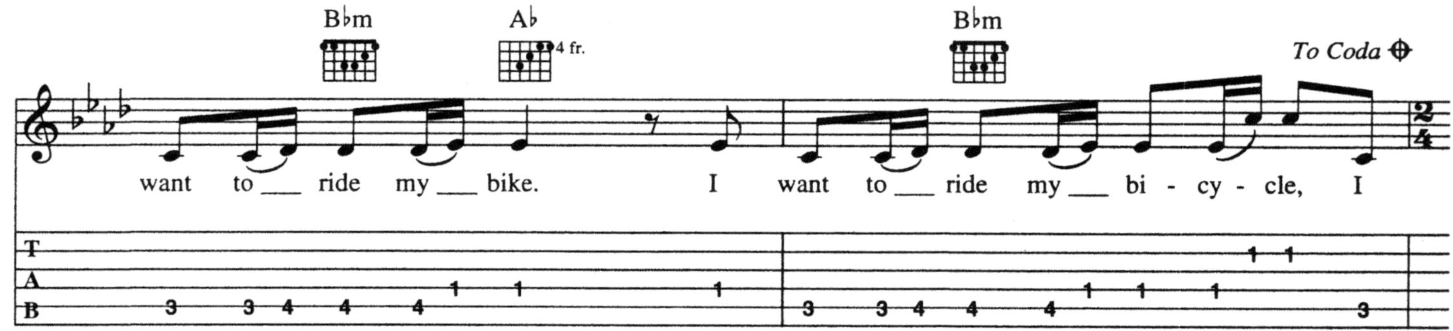
B♭m
A♭
4 fr.
B♭m
To Coda
want to ___ ride my ___ bike. I want to ___ ride my ___ bi - cy - cle, I
T
A
B

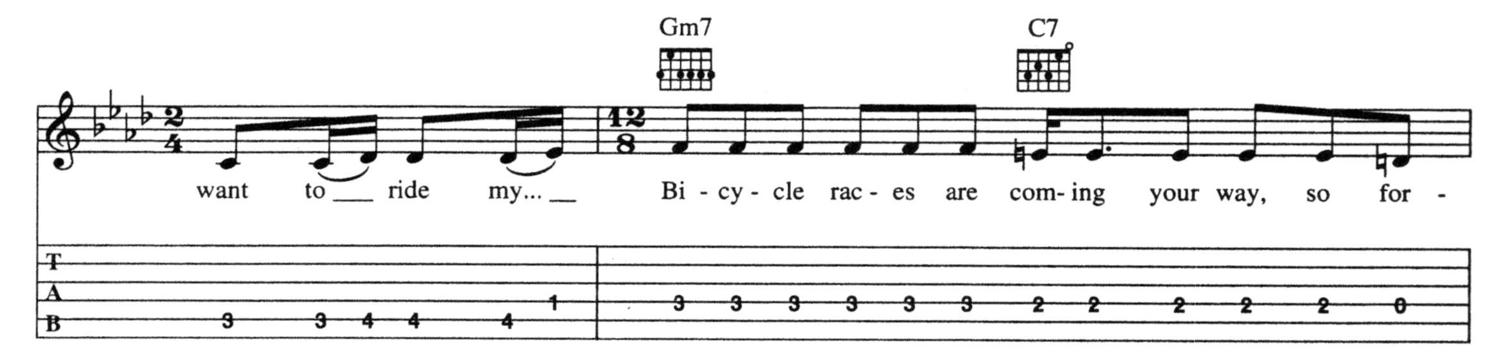
Gm7
C7
want to ___ ride my... ___ Bi - cy - cle rac - es are com - ing your way, so for -
T
A
B

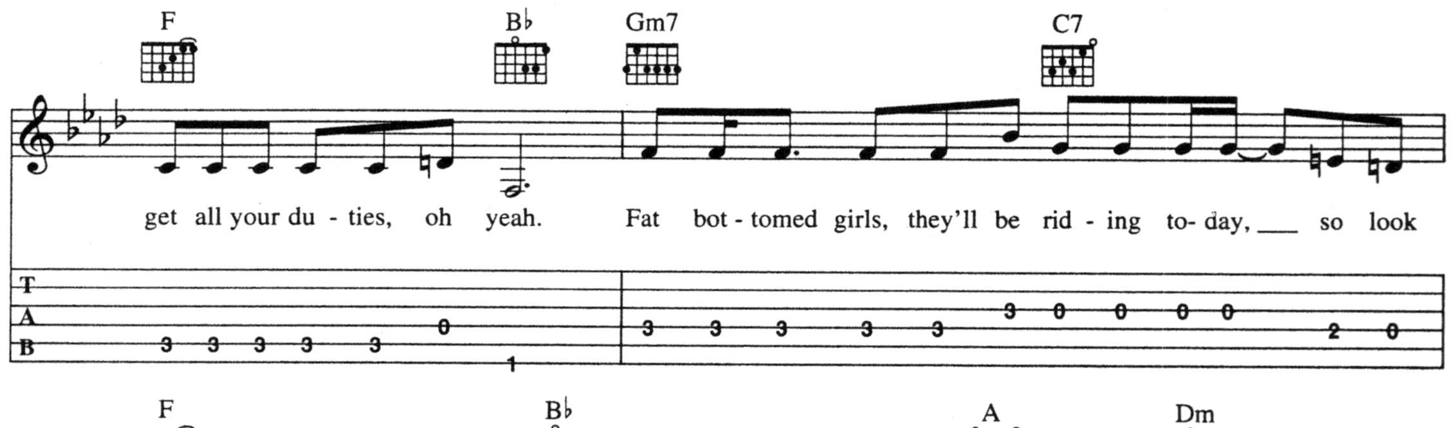
F
B♭
Gm7
C7
get all your du - ties, oh yeah. Fat bot - tomed girls, they'll be rid - ing to - day, ___ so look
T
A
B

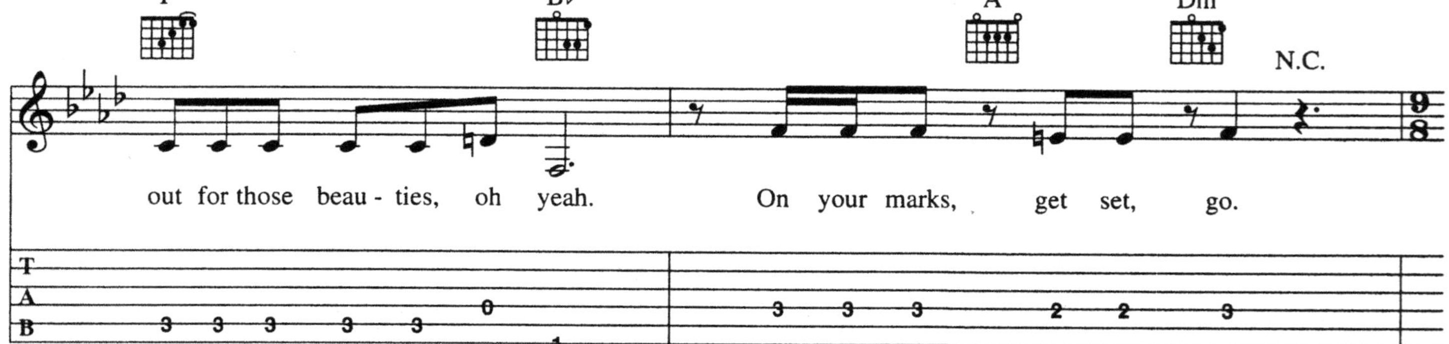
F
B♭
A
Dm
N.C.
out for those beau - ties, oh yeah. On your marks, get set, go.
T
A
B

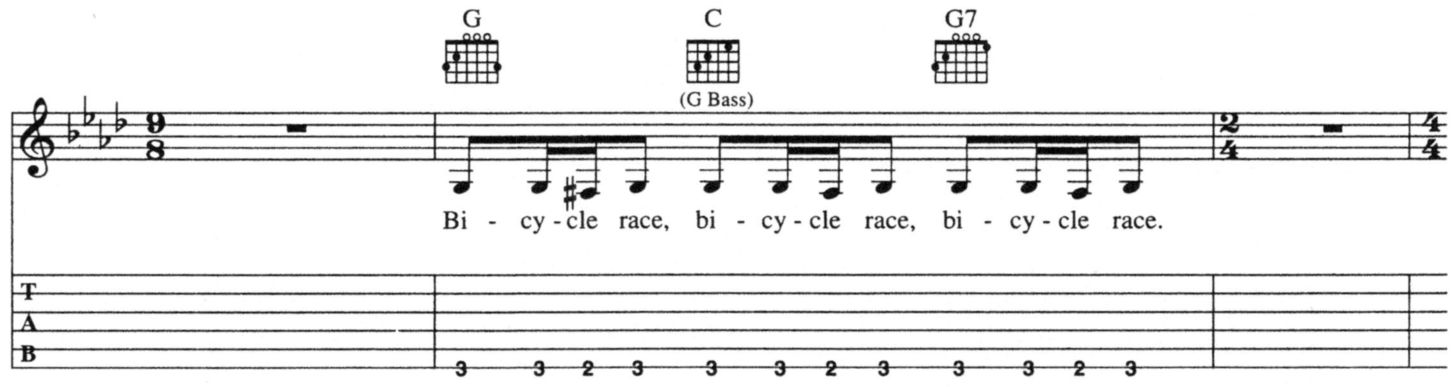
G
C
G7
(G Bass)
Bi - cy - cle race, bi - cy - cle race, bi - cy - cle race.
T
A
B

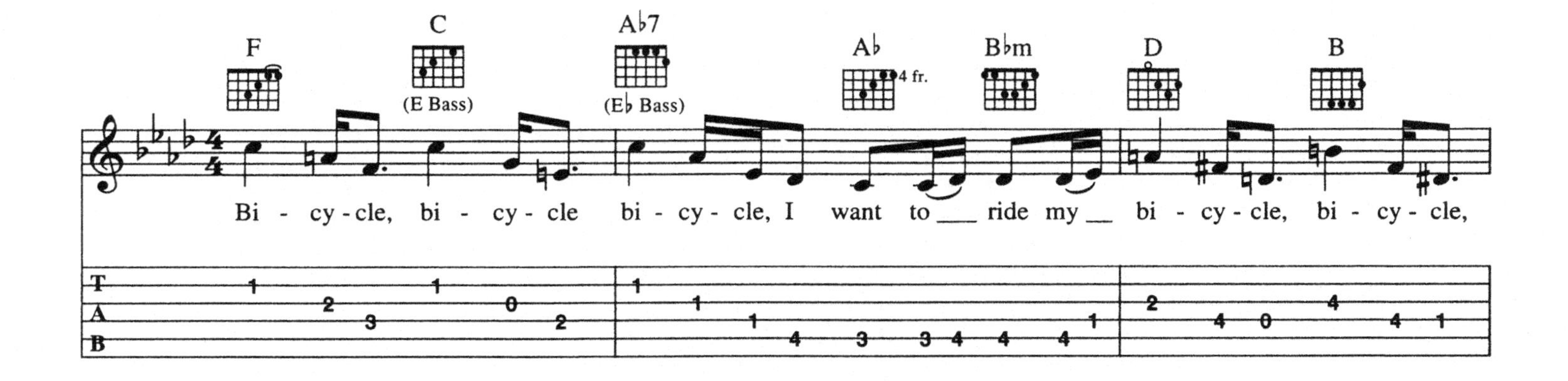
F
C
A♭7
A♭
B♭m
D
B
4 fr.
(E Bass)
(E♭ Bass)
Bi - cy - cle, bi - cy - cle bi - cy - cle, I want to ___ ride my __ bi - cy - cle, bi - cy - cle,
T
A
B

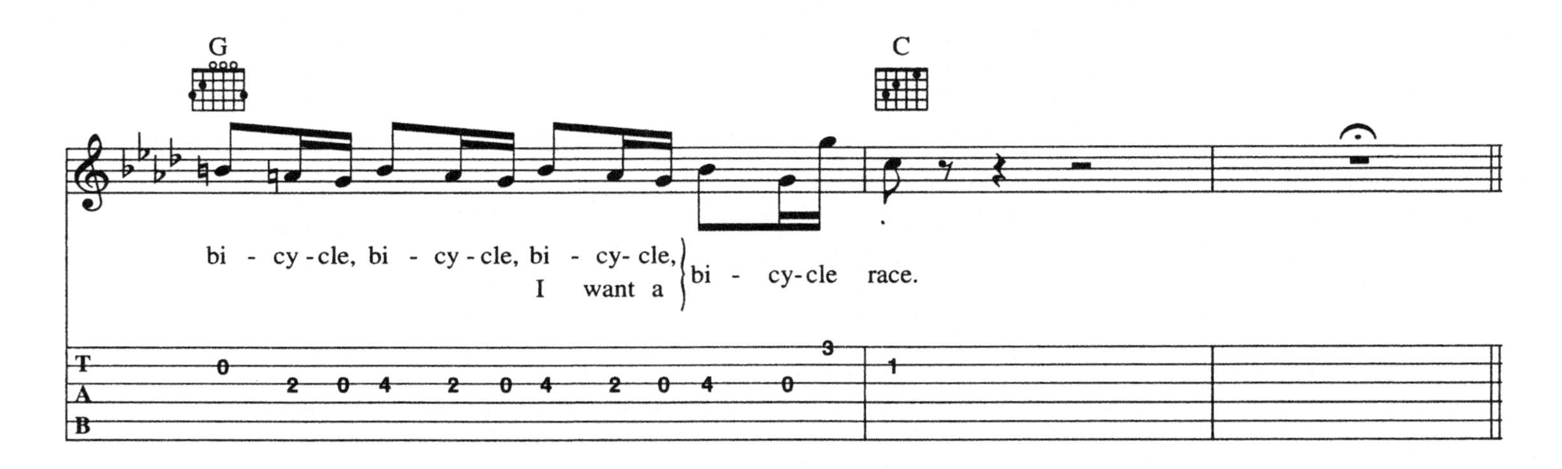
G
C
bi - cy - cle, bi - cy - cle, bi - cy - cle,
I want a
bi - cy - cle race.
T
A
B

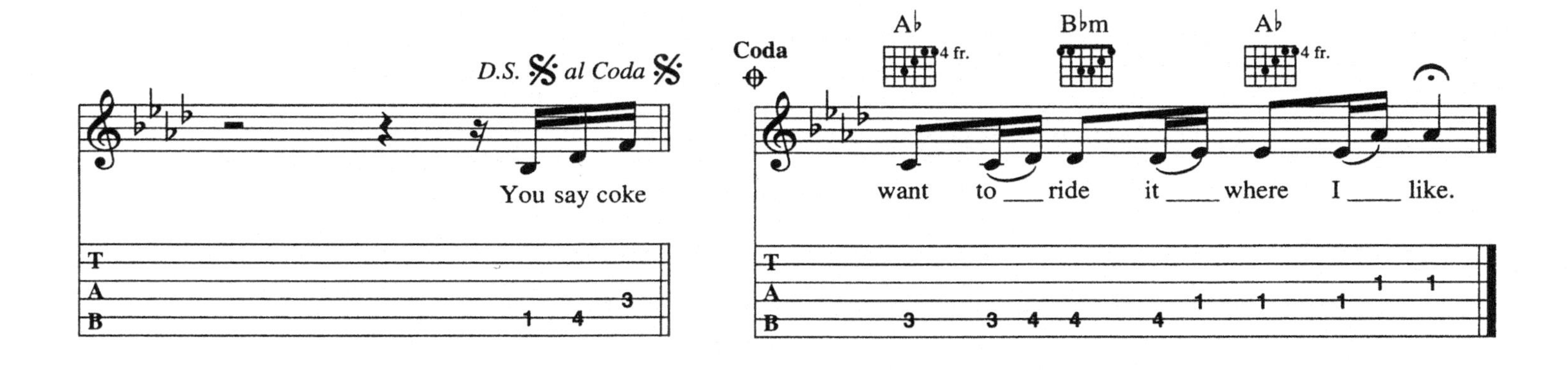
D.S. al Coda
You say coke
Coda
A♭
B♭m
A♭
4 fr.
4 fr.
want to ___ ride it ____ where I ____ like.
T
A
B

# BODY LANGUAGE

Words and Music by
FREDDIE MERCURY

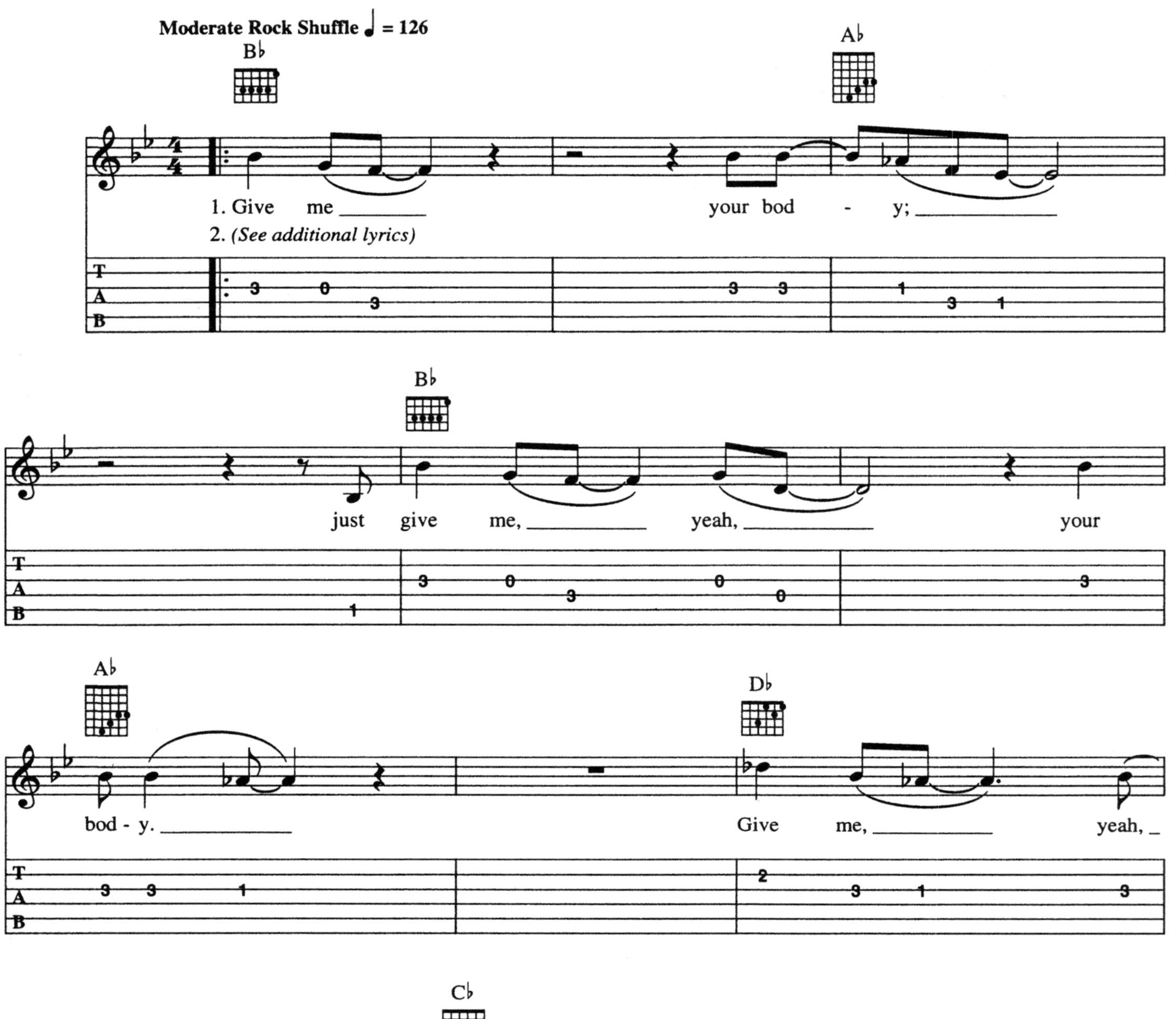


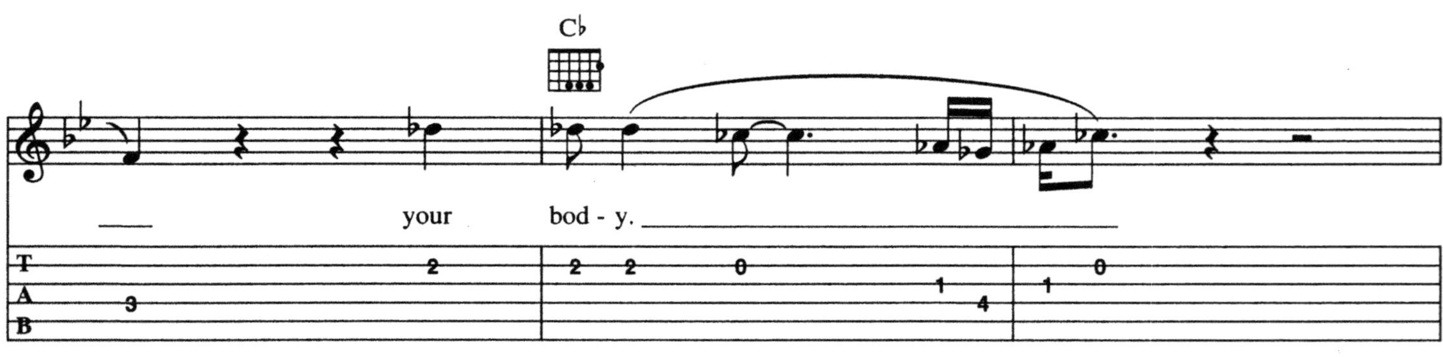

E♭
Don't talk.
E♭7sus
Bod - y lan - guage,
bod - y lan - guage,
1.
2.
D9
bod - y lan - guage.
bod - y lan - guage.
B♭
You got
red
lips;
A♭
snakes
in your
eyes;
B♭
long
legs;

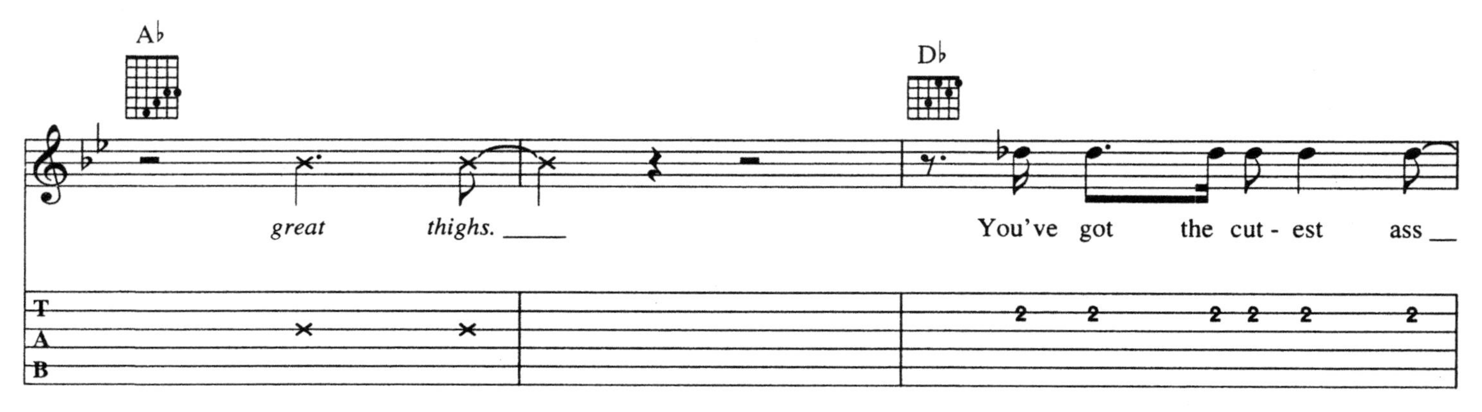
A♭
D♭
great thighs.
You've got the cut - est ass

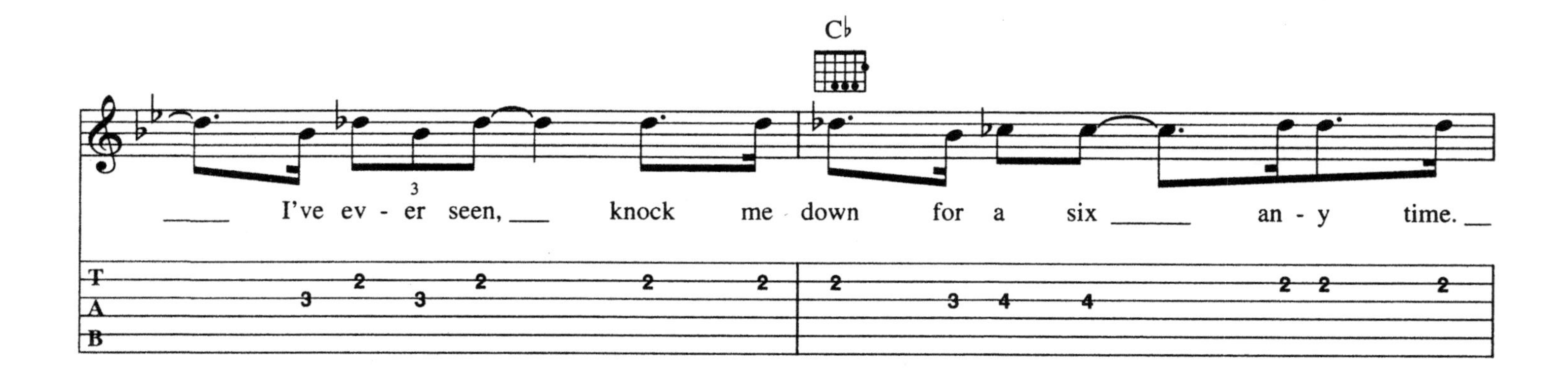
C♭
I've ev - er seen, knock me down for a six an - y time.

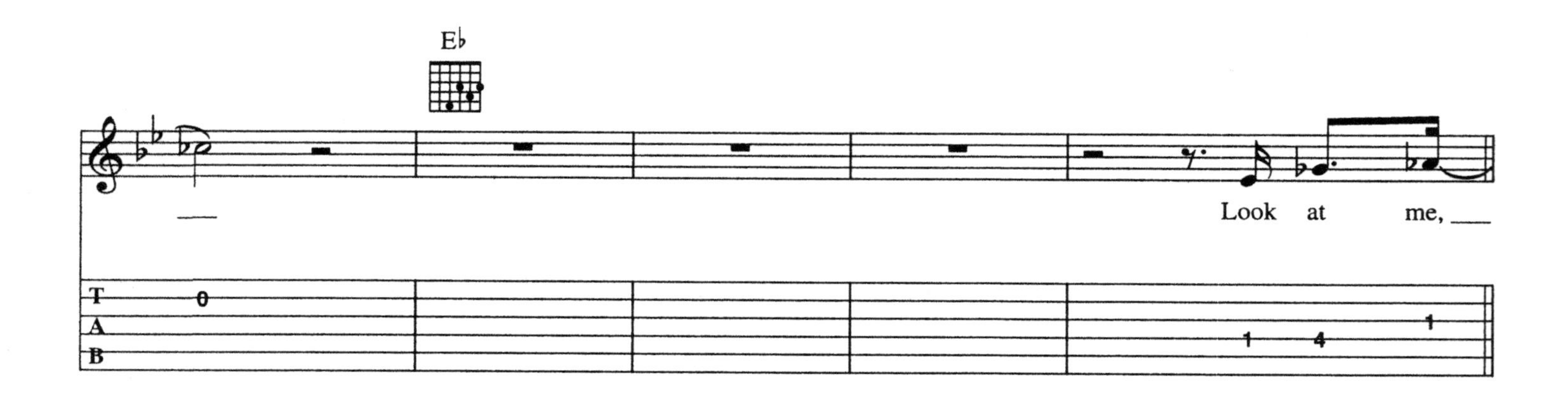
E♭
Look at me,

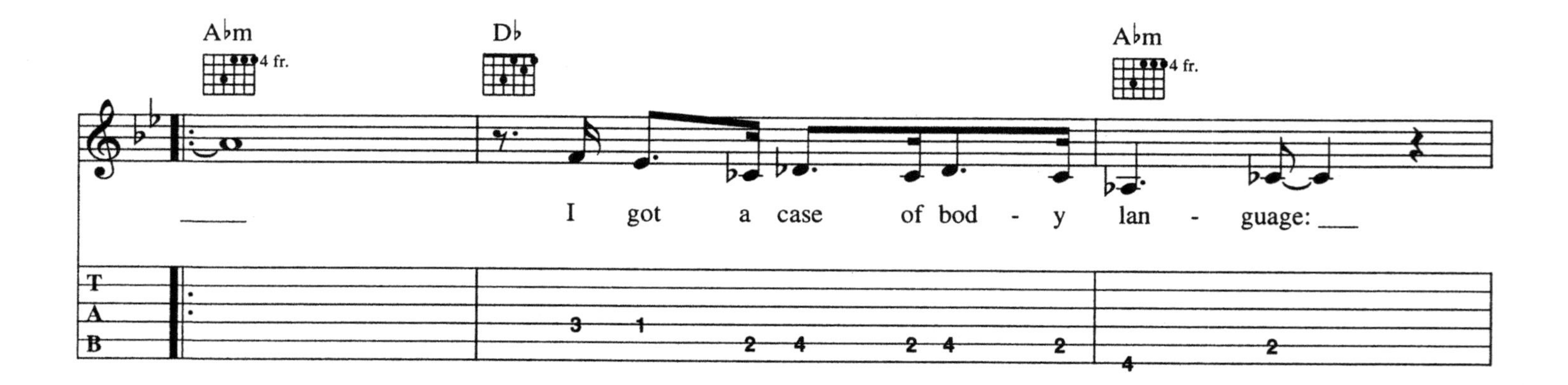
A♭m
4 fr.
D♭
A♭m
4 fr.
I got a case of bod - y lan - guage:

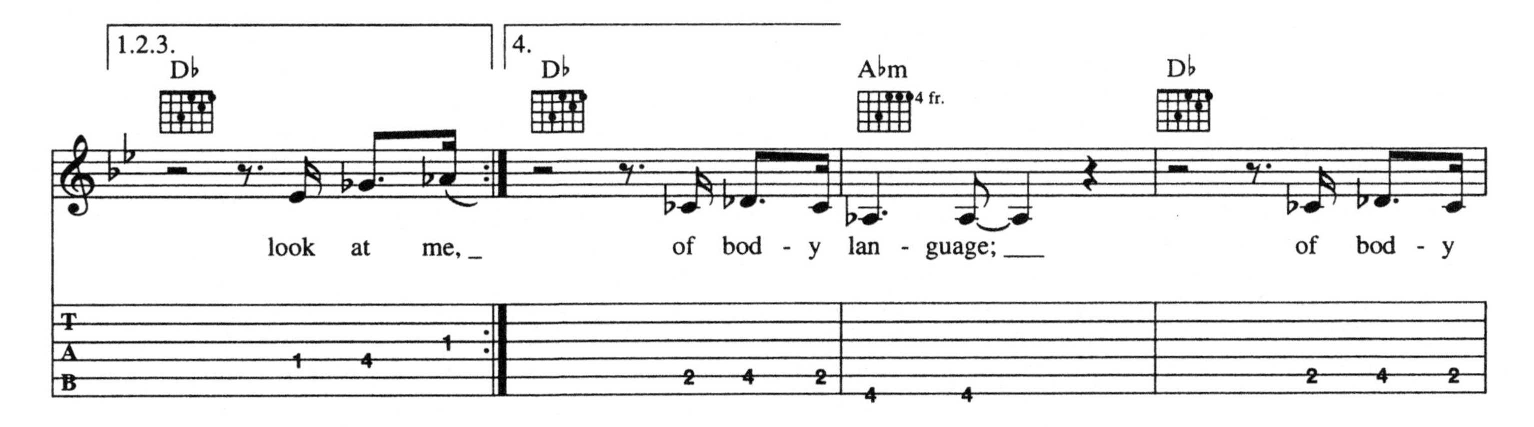


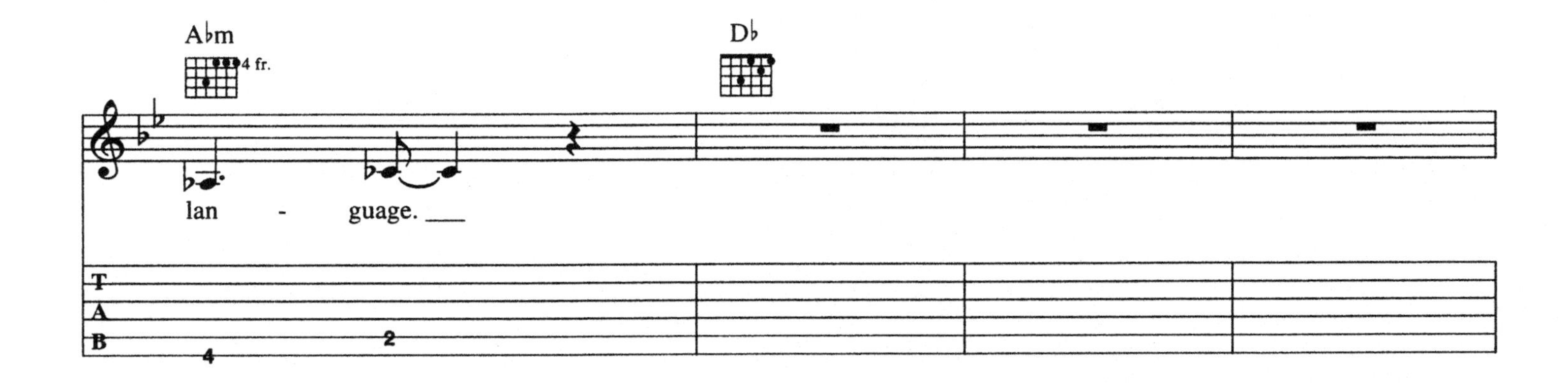


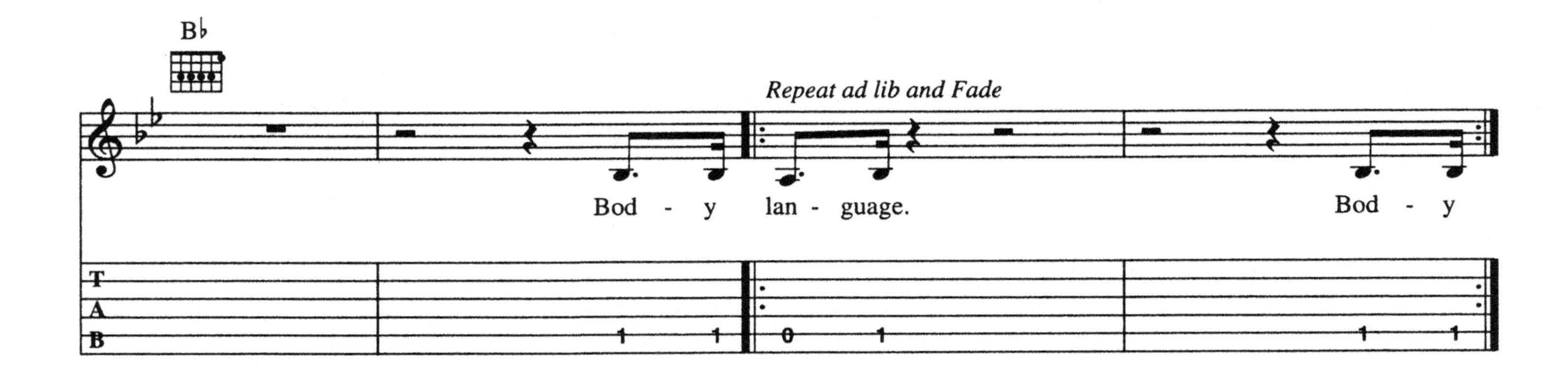


2. *Sexy body;*
*Sexy,* sexy body.
I want your body.
*Baby, you're hot!*

*(To Coda)*

# BOHEMIAN RHAPSODY

Words and Music by
FREDDIE MERCURY

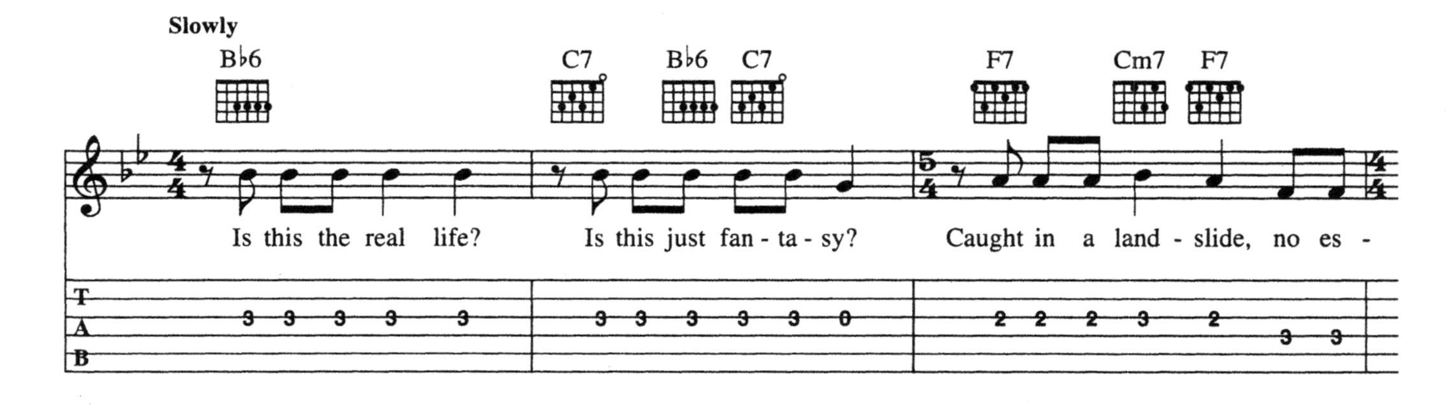


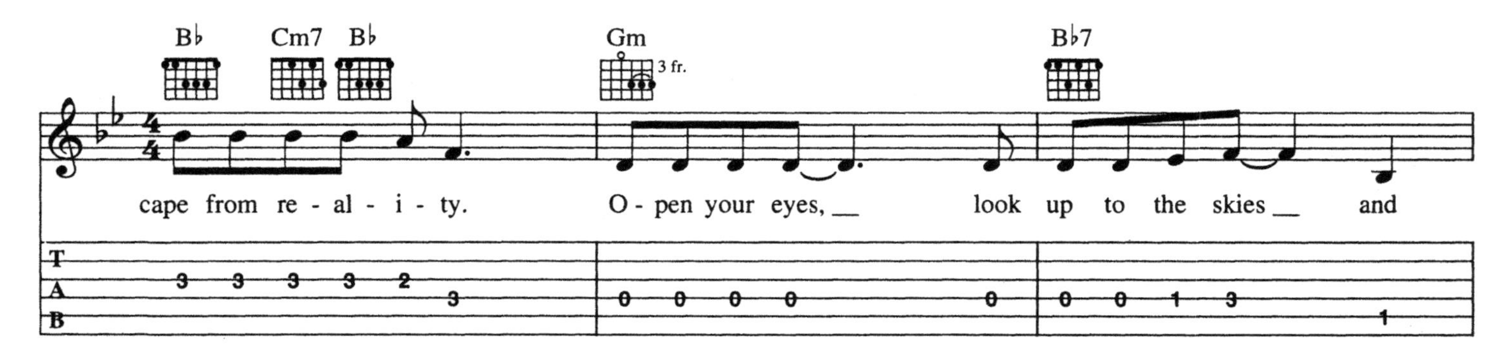


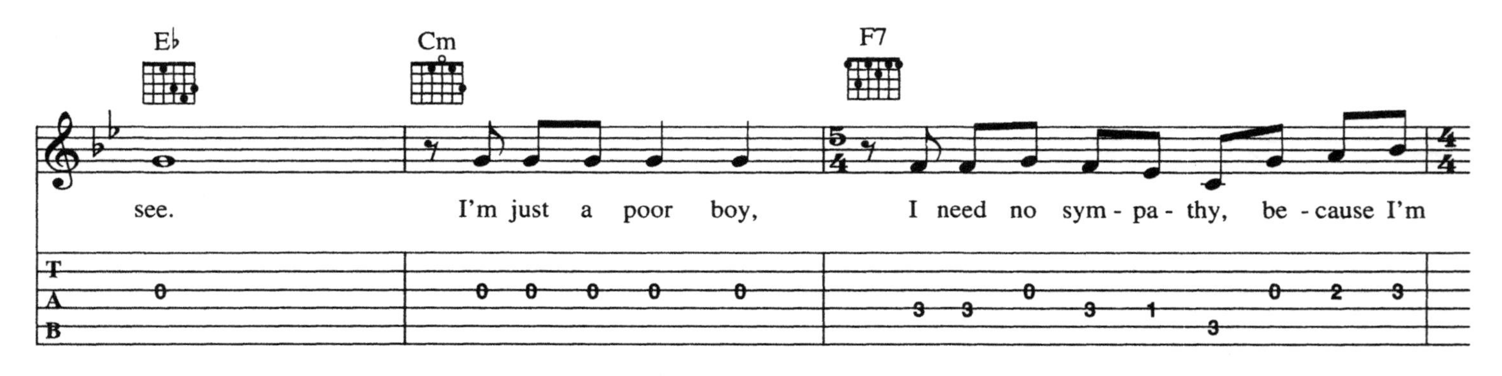


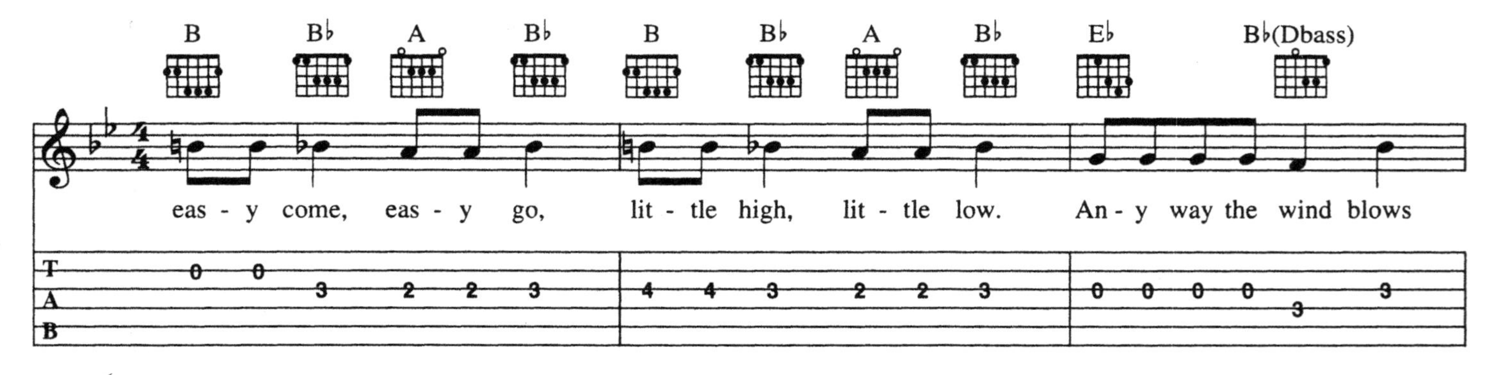

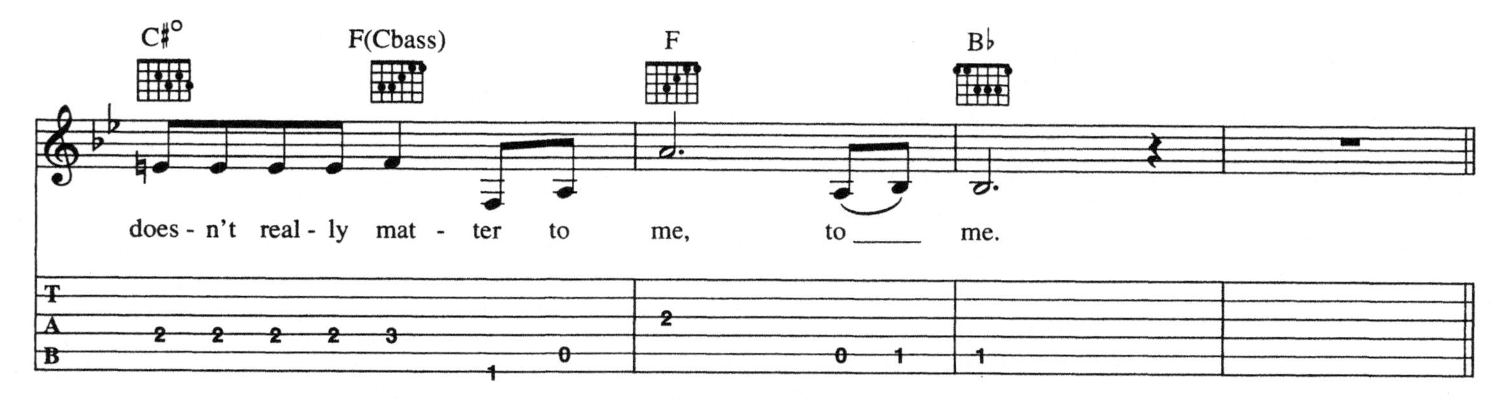
C♯°
F(Cbass)
F
B♭
does - n't real - ly mat - ter to me, to ____ me.
T
A
B

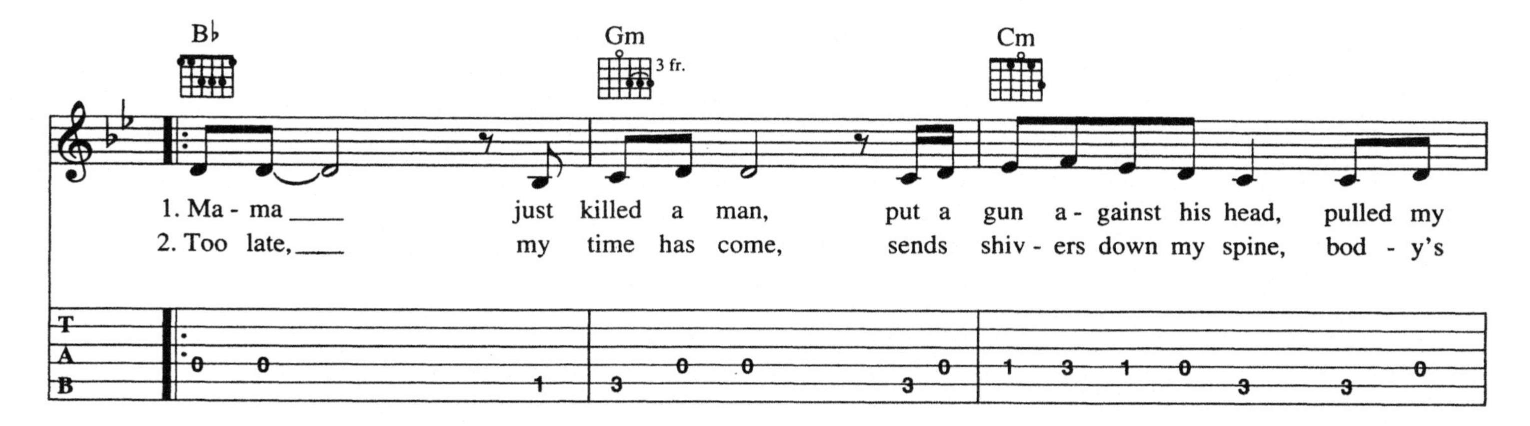
B♭
Gm
3 fr.
Cm
1. Ma - ma ____ just killed a man, put a gun a - gainst his head, pulled my
2. Too late, ____ my time has come, sends shiv - ers down my spine, bod - y's
T
A
B

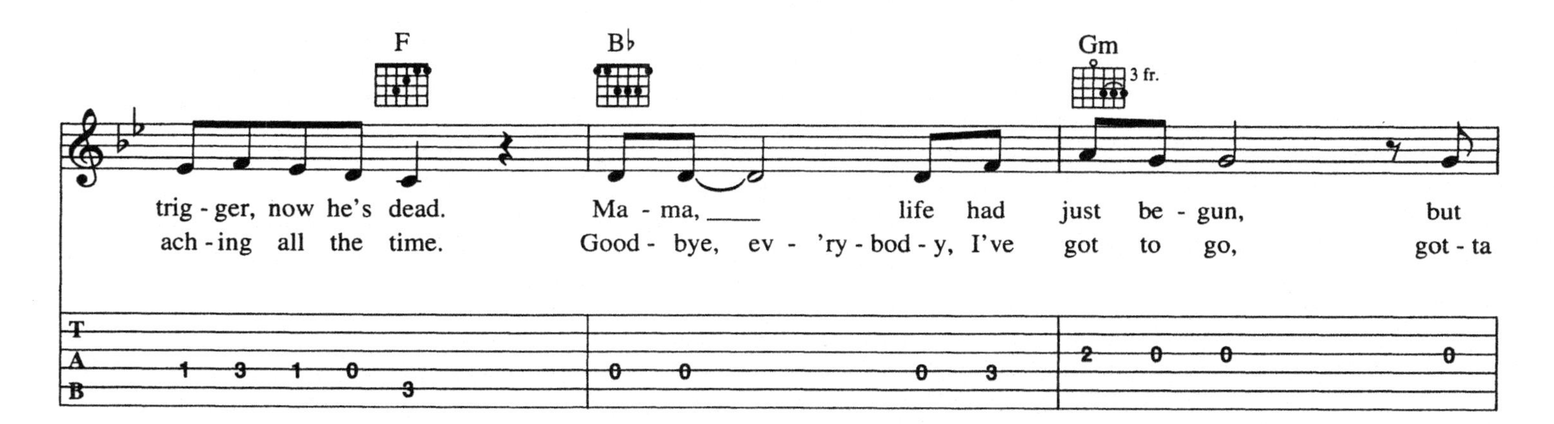
F
B♭
Gm
3 fr.
trig - ger, now he's dead. Ma - ma, ____ life had just be - gun, but
ach - ing all the time. Good - bye, ev - 'ry - bod - y, I've got to go, got - ta
T
A
B

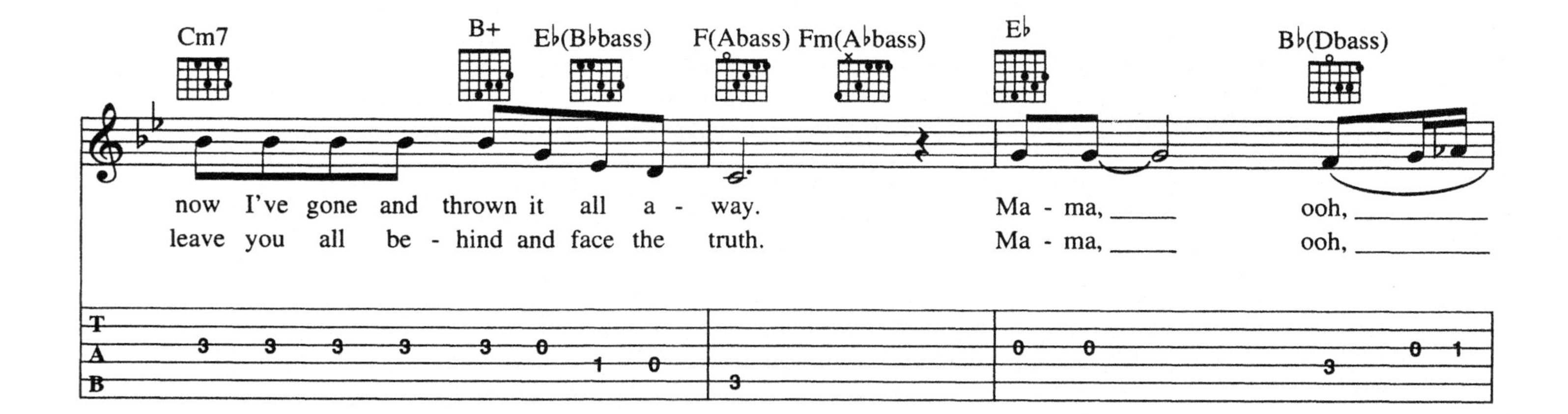
Cm7
B+
E♭(B♭bass)
F(Abass)
Fm(A♭bass)
E♭
B♭(Dbass)
now I've gone and thrown it all a - way. Ma - ma, ____ ooh, ____
leave you all be - hind and face the truth. Ma - ma, ____ ooh, ____
T
A
B

Cm
Fm
B♭
did - n't mean to make you cry. If I'm not back a - gain this time to -
I don't want to die, I some - times wish I'd nev - er been born at

1.
E♭
B♭(Dbass)
Cm
A♭m
4 fr.
E♭
A♭
4 fr.
E♭
mor - row, car - ry on, car - ry on as if noth - ing real - ly mat - ters.

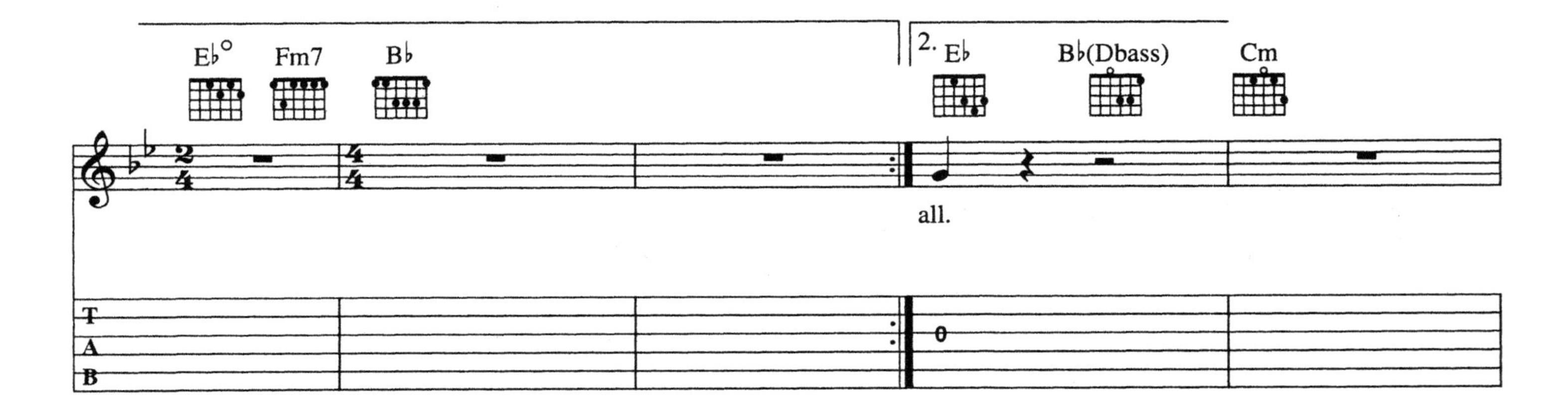
E♭°
Fm7
B♭
2.
E♭
B♭(Dbass)
Cm
all.

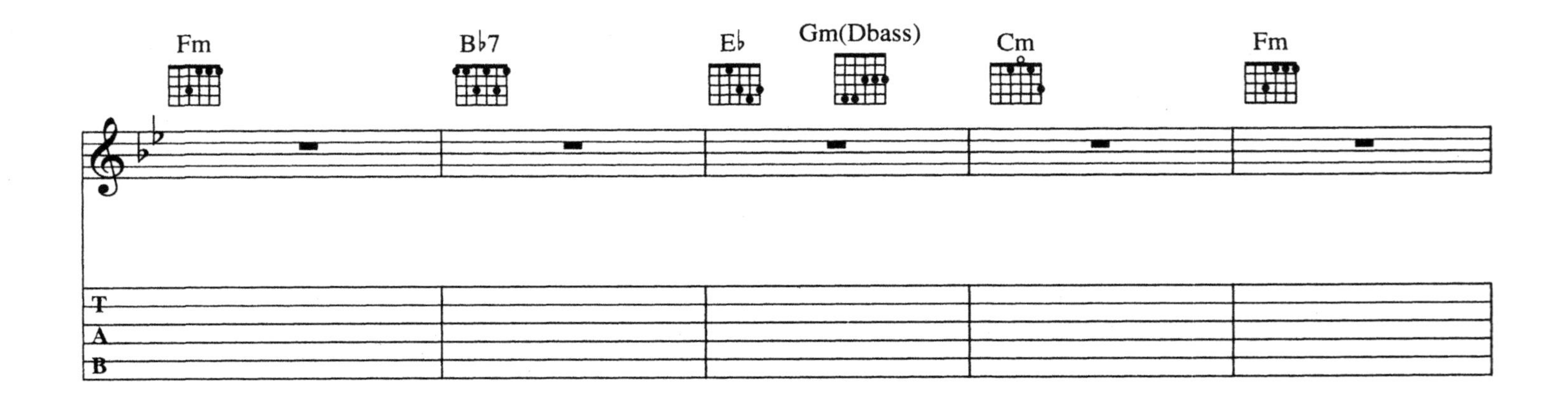
Fm
B♭7
E♭
Gm(Dbass)
Cm
Fm

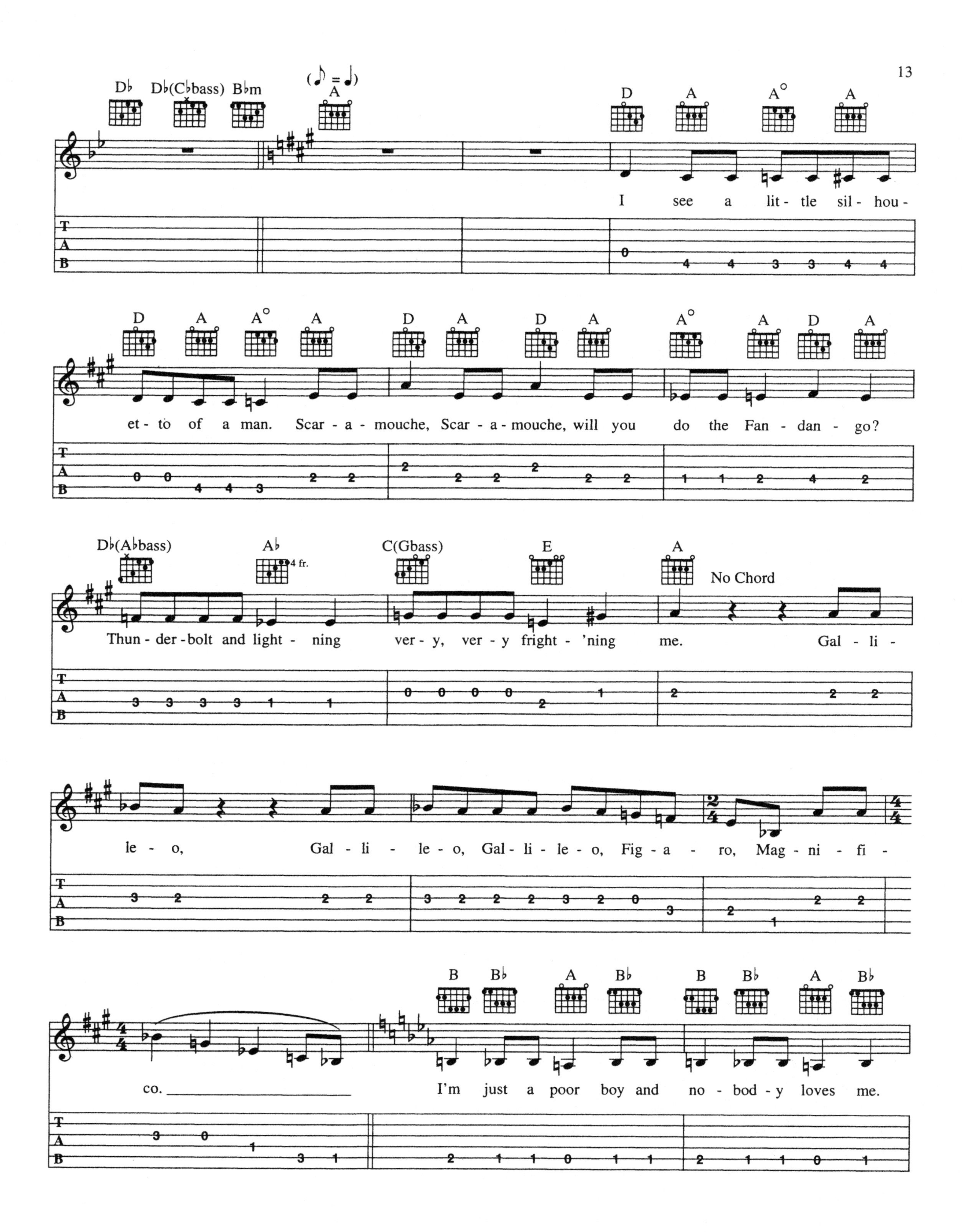

D♭ D♭(C♭bass) B♭m
(♪ = ♩)
A
D A A° A
I see a lit - tle sil - hou -
D A A° A D A D A A° A D A
et - to of a man. Scar - a - mouche, Scar - a - mouche, will you do the Fan - dan - go?
D♭(A♭bass) A♭ 4 fr. C(Gbass) E A
No Chord
Thun - der - bolt and light - ning ver - y, ver - y fright - 'ning me. Gal - li -
le - o, Gal - li - le - o, Gal - li - le - o, Fig - a - ro, Mag - ni - fi -
B B♭ A B♭ B B♭ A B♭
co. I'm just a poor boy and no - bod - y loves me.
T
A
B

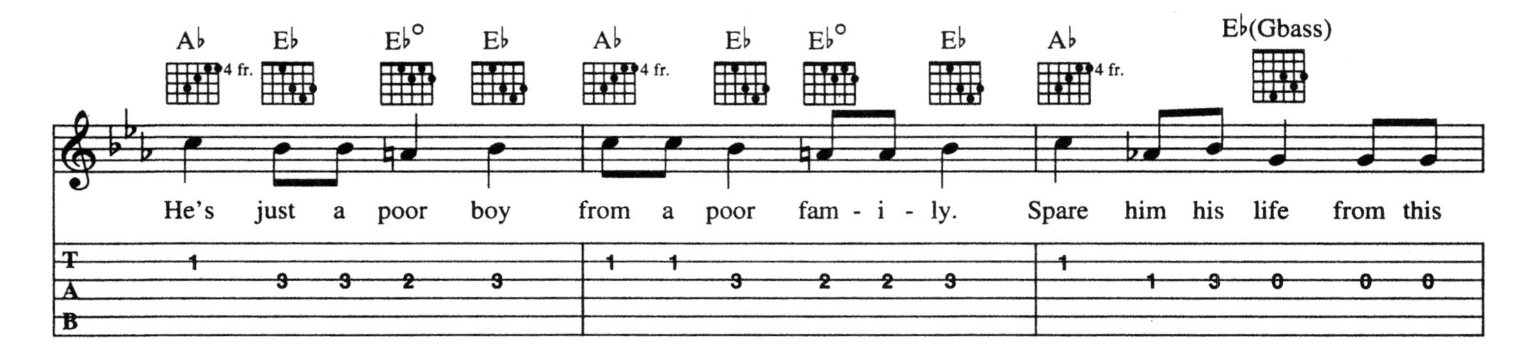
A♭ E♭ E♭° E♭ A♭ E♭ E♭° E♭ A♭ E♭(Gbass)
4 fr.
He's just a poor boy from a poor fam - i - ly. Spare him his life from this

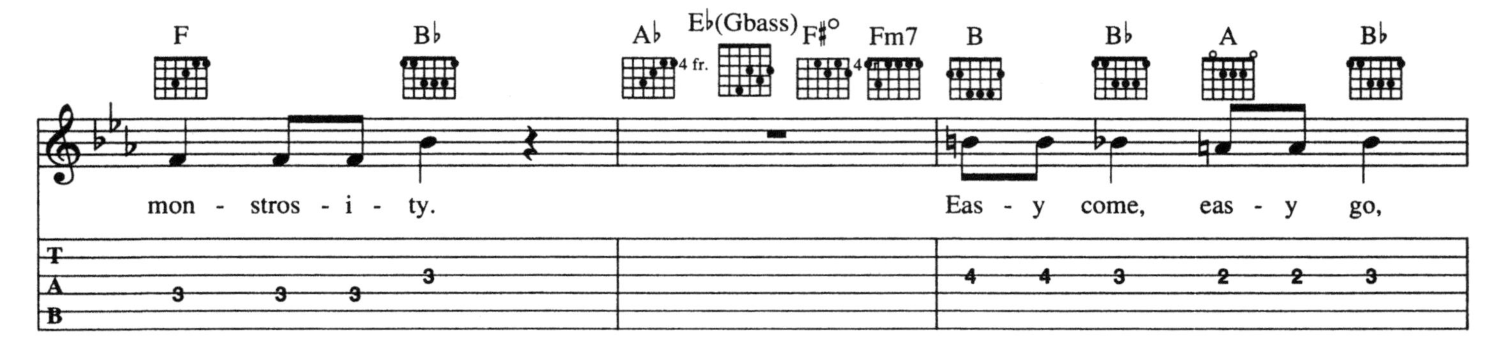
F B♭ A♭ E♭(Gbass) F♯° Fm7 B B♭ A B♭
4 fr.
mon - stros - i - ty. Eas - y come, eas - y go,

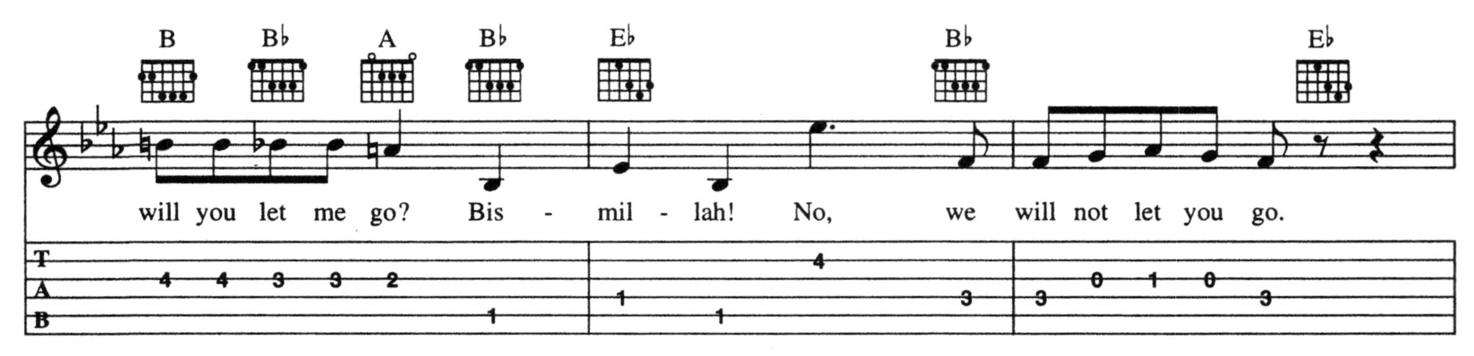
B B♭ A B♭ E♭ B♭ E♭
will you let me go? Bis - mil - lah! No, we will not let you go.

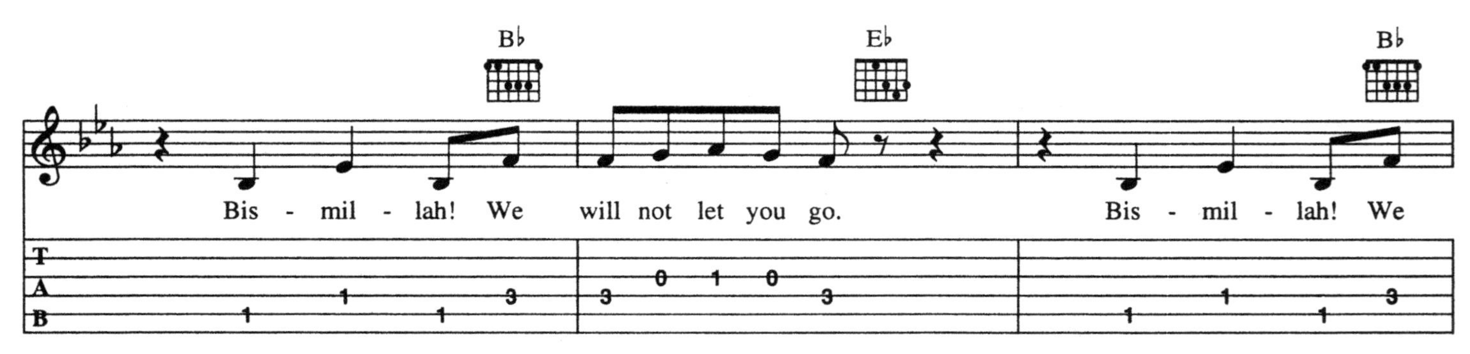
B♭ E♭ B♭
Bis - mil - lah! We will not let you go. Bis - mil - lah! We

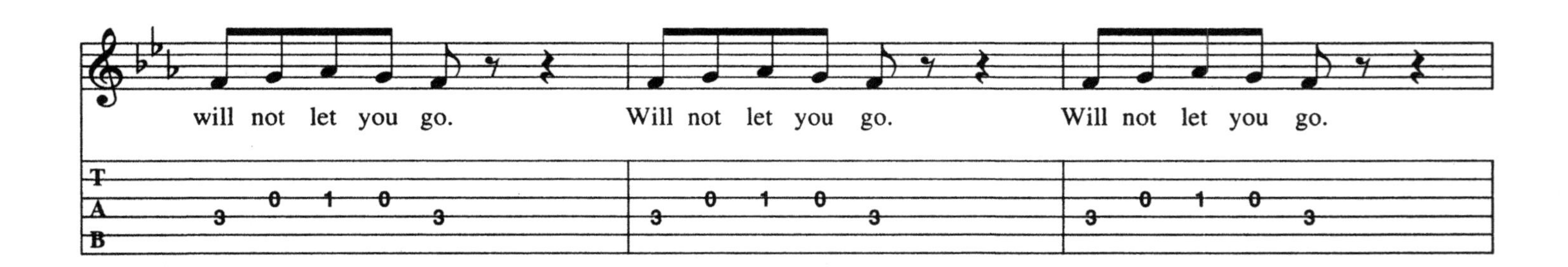
will not let you go. Will not let you go. Will not let you go.

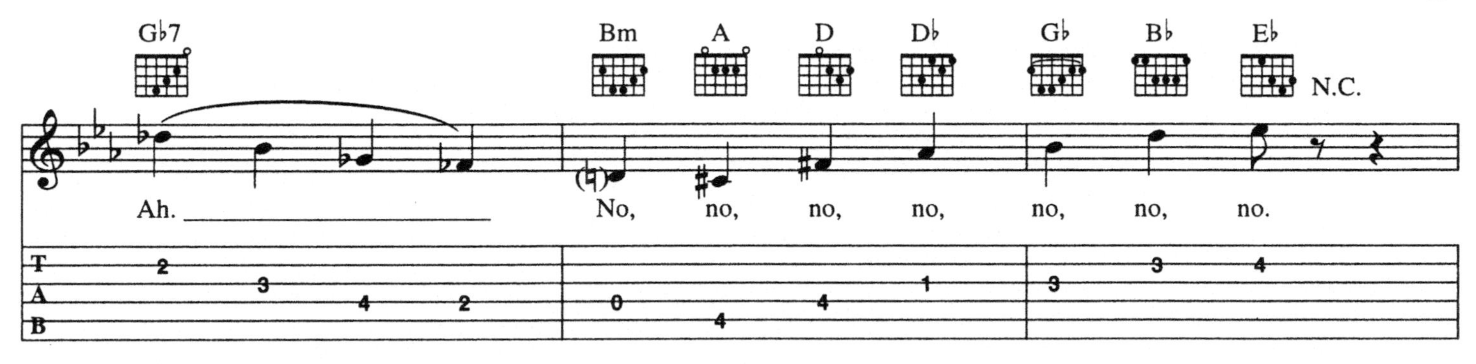
G♭7
Bm
A
D
D♭
G♭
B♭
E♭
N.C.
Ah.
No, no, no, no, no, no, no.

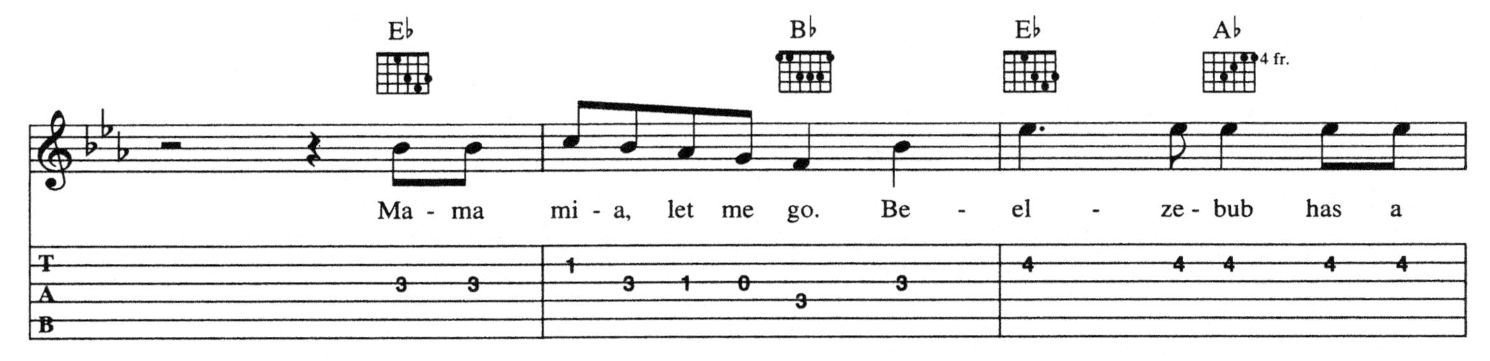
E♭
B♭
E♭
A♭
4 fr.
Ma - ma mi - a, let me go. Be - el - ze - bub has a

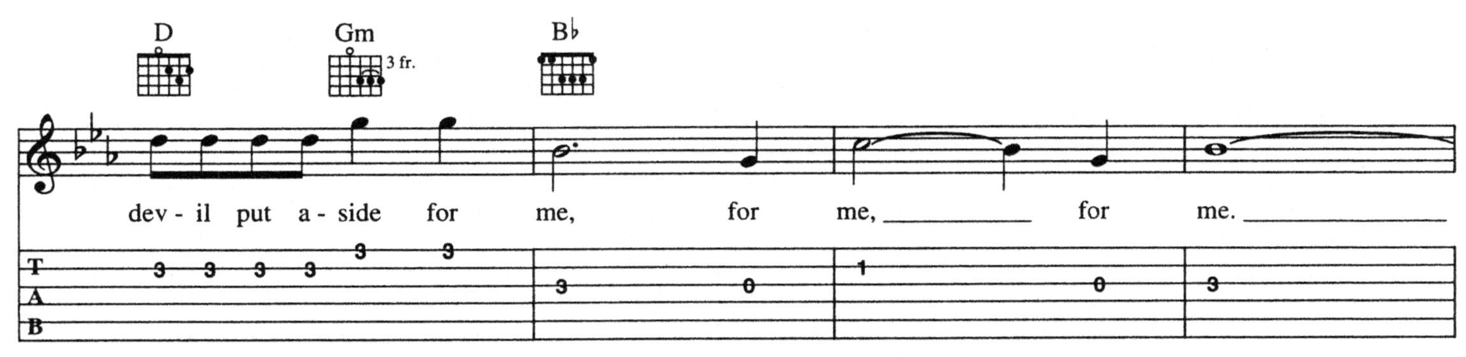
D
Gm
3 fr.
B♭
dev - il put a - side for me, for me, for me.

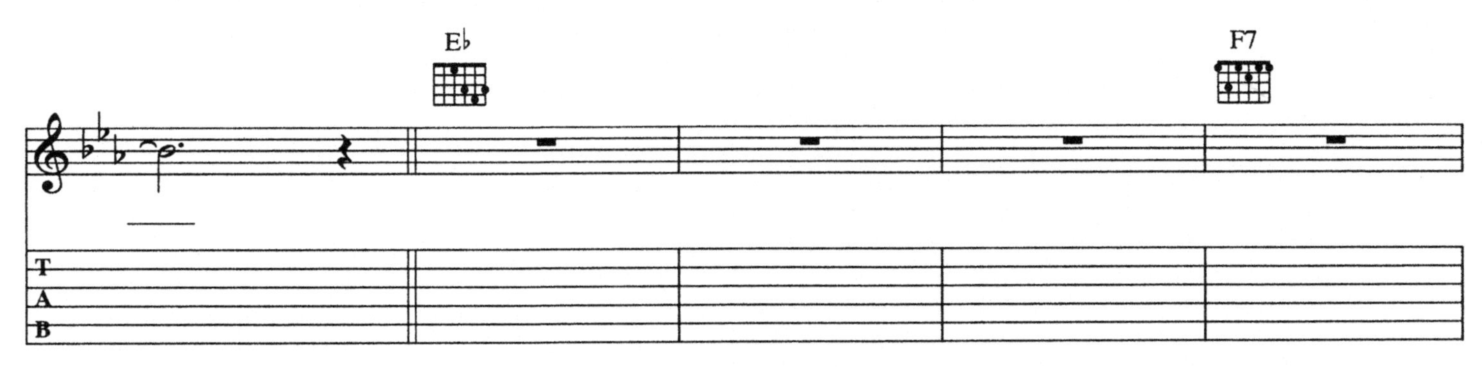
E♭
F7

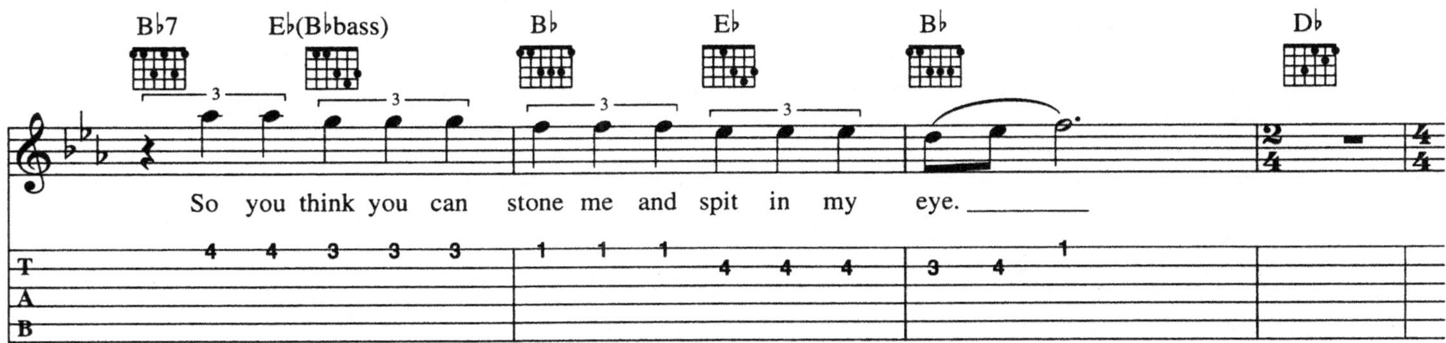
B♭7
E♭(B♭bass)
B♭
E♭
B♭
D♭
So you think you can stone me and spit in my eye.

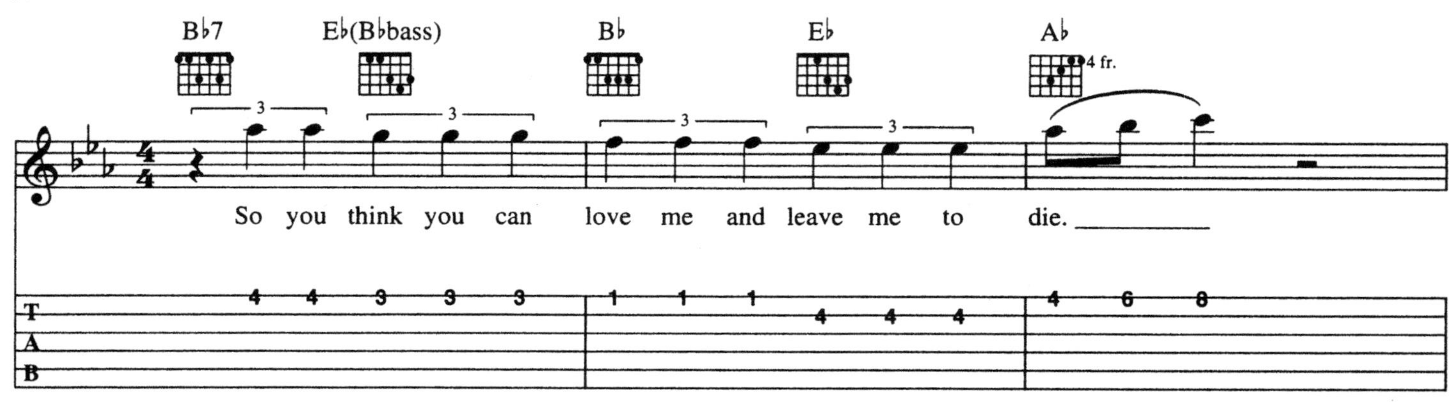
B♭7
E♭(B♭bass)
B♭
E♭
A♭
4 fr.
So you think you can love me and leave me to die.

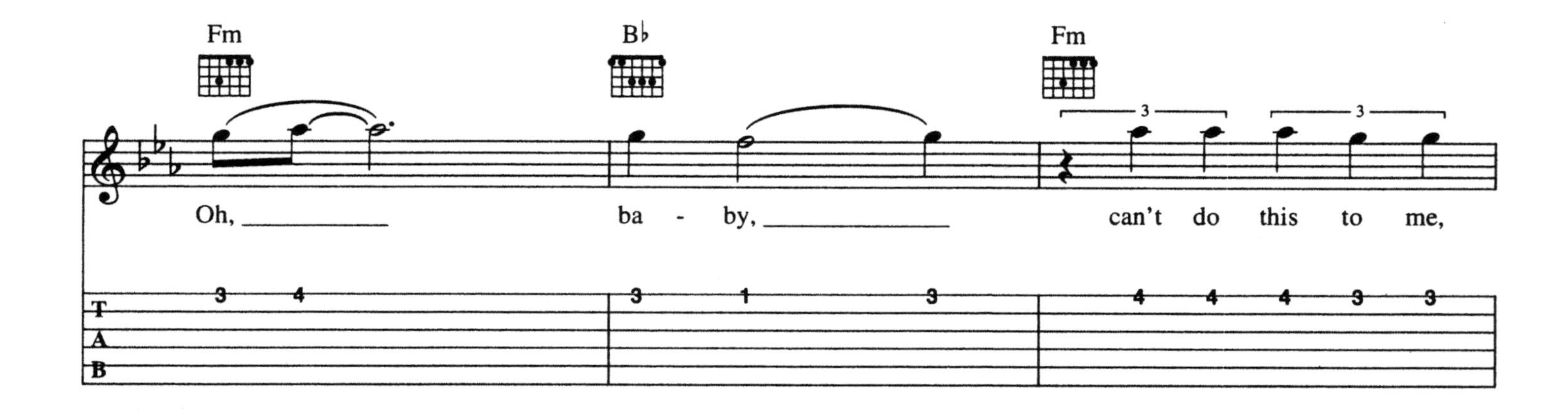
Fm
B♭
Fm
Oh, ba - by, can't do this to me,

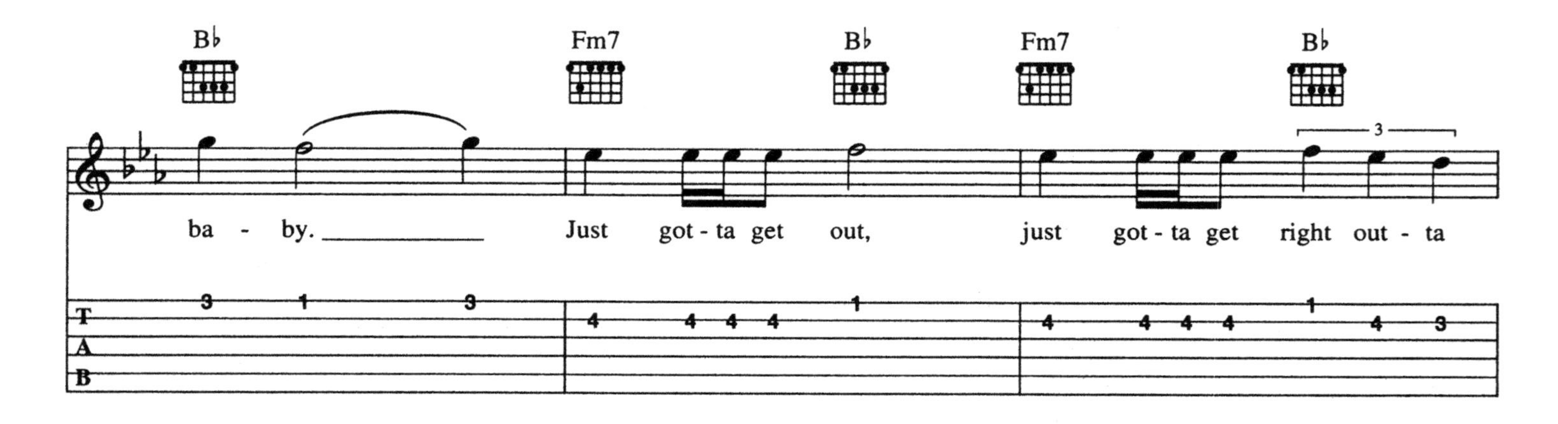
B♭
Fm7
B♭
Fm7
B♭
ba - by. Just got - ta get out, just got - ta get right out - ta

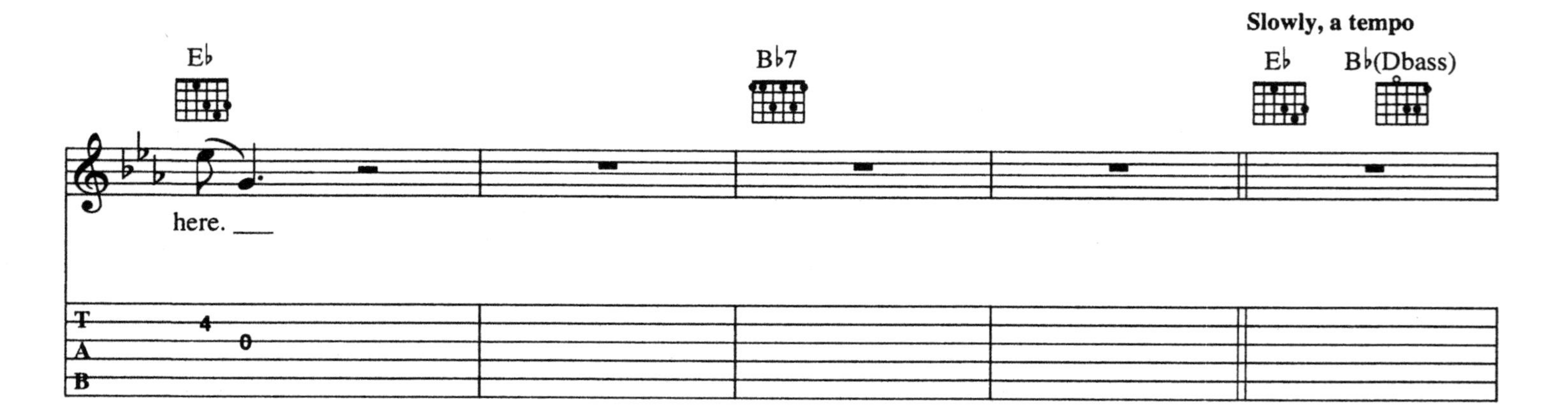
Slowly, a tempo
E♭
B♭7
E♭
B♭(Dbass)
here.

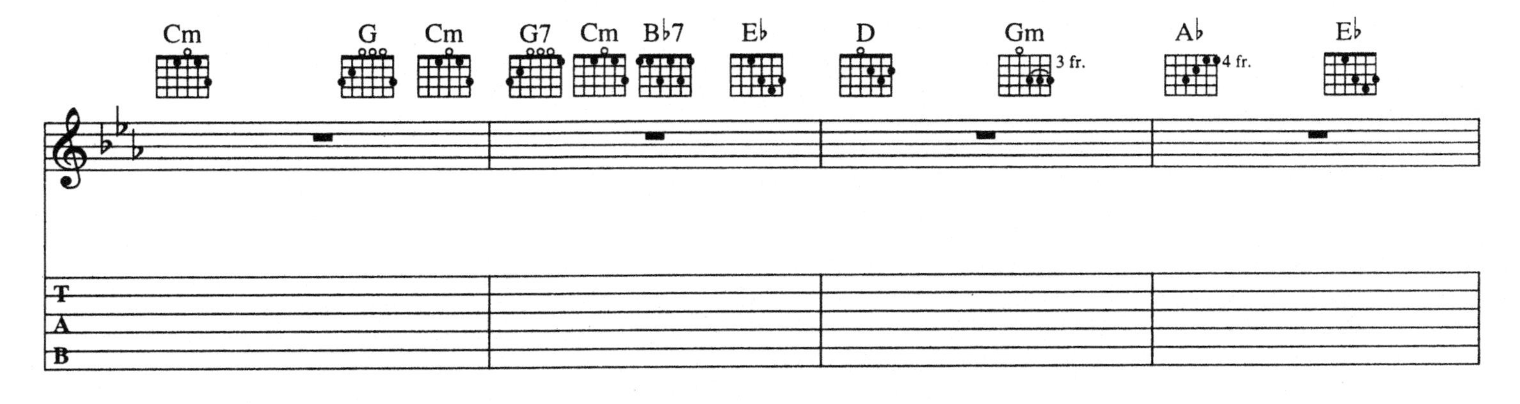
Cm
G
Cm
G7
Cm
B♭7
E♭
D
Gm
3 fr.
A♭
4 fr.
E♭

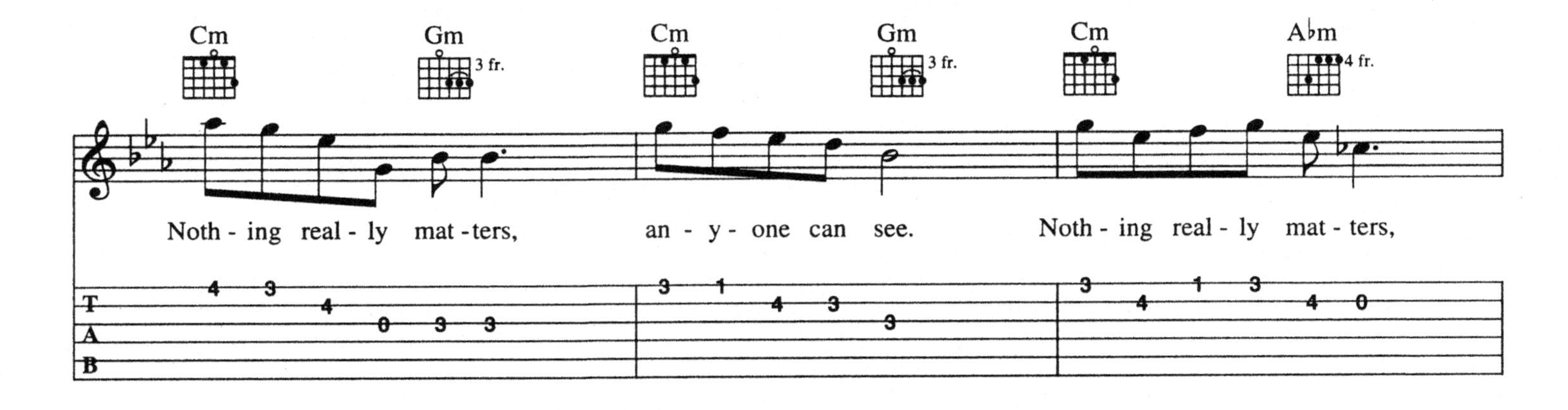
Cm
Gm
3 fr.
Cm
Gm
3 fr.
Cm
A♭m
4 fr.
Noth - ing real - ly mat - ters, an - y - one can see. Noth - ing real - ly mat - ters,

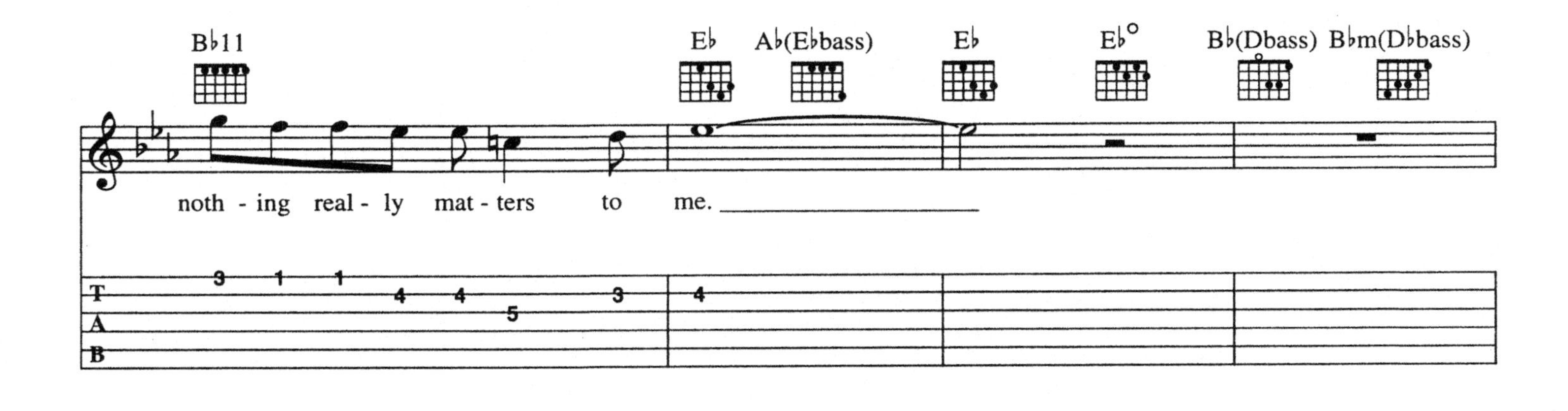
B♭11
E♭
A♭(E♭bass)
E♭
E♭°
B♭(Dbass)
B♭m(D♭bass)
noth - ing real - ly mat - ters to me.

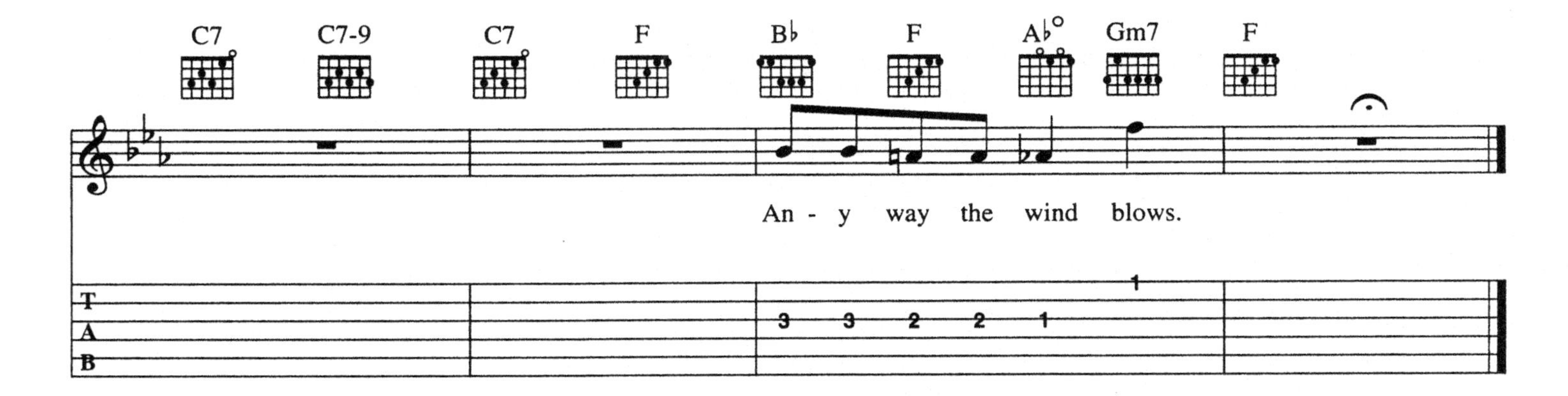
C7
C7-9
C7
F
B♭
F
A♭°
Gm7
F
An - y way the wind blows.

# CRAZY LITTLE THING CALLED LOVE

Words and Music by
FREDDIE MERCURY

G
C
G
D
___ (like a baby) in a cra - dle all night, ___ it swings, ___ it jives, _
T
A
B

G
C
G
___ it shakes all o - ver like a jel - ly fish, ___ I kind - a
T
A
B

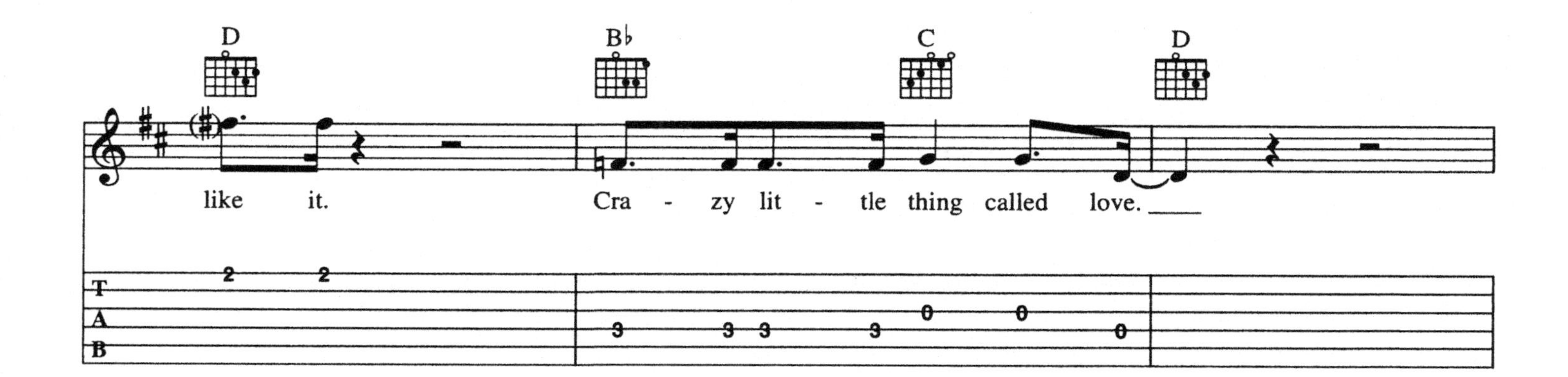
D
B♭
C
D
like it. Cra - zy lit - tle thing called love. ___
T
A
B

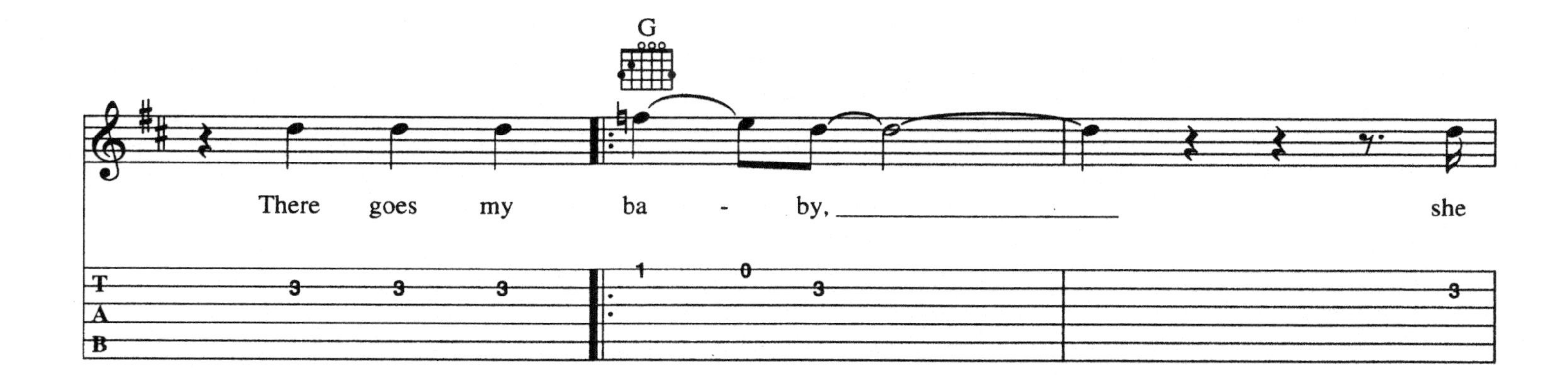
G
There goes my ba - by, ___ she
T
A
B

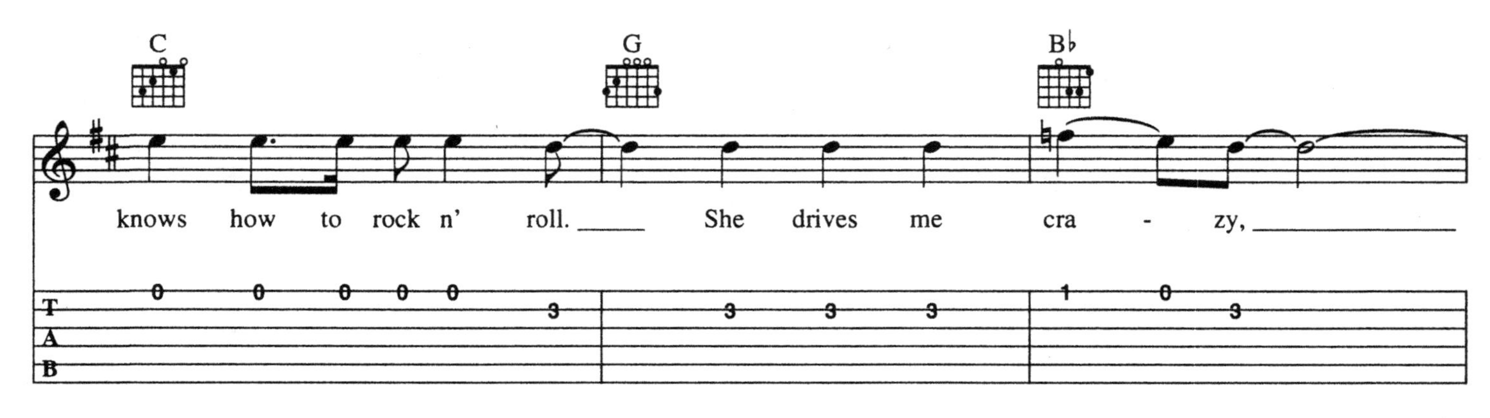
C
G
B♭
knows how to rock n' roll. She drives me cra - zy,

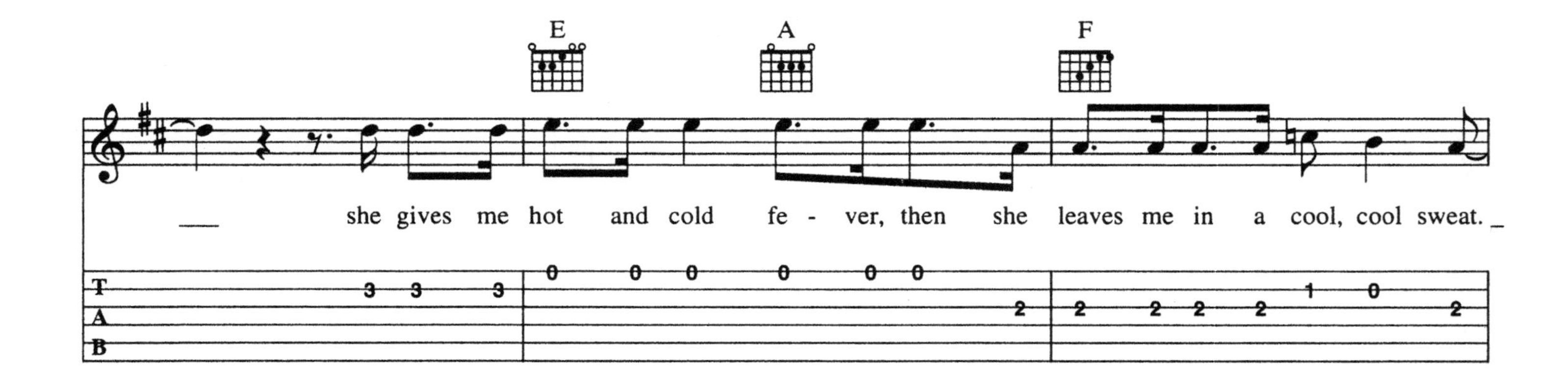
E
A
F
she gives me hot and cold fe - ver, then she leaves me in a cool, cool sweat.

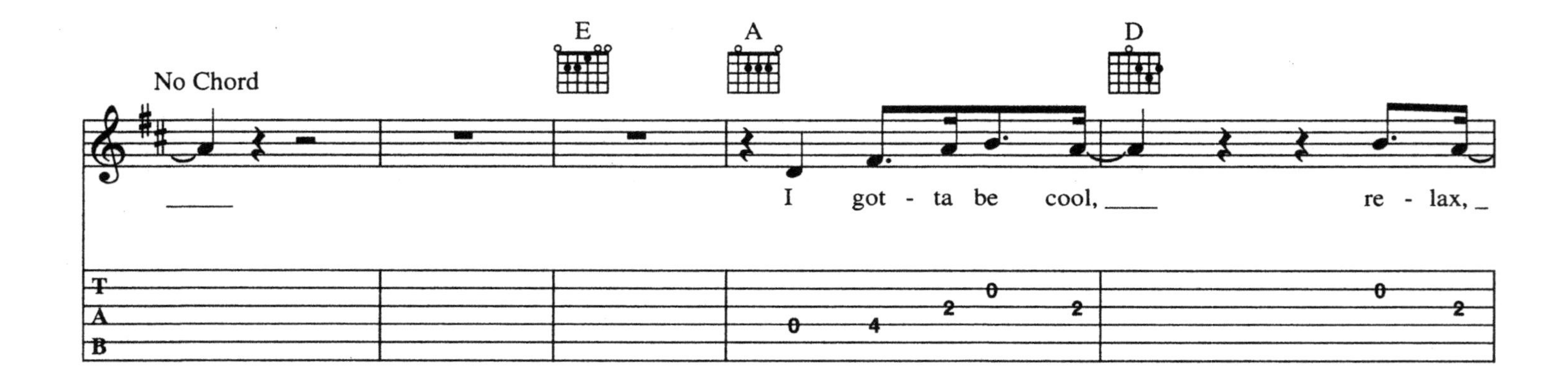
No Chord
E
A
D
I got - ta be cool, re - lax,

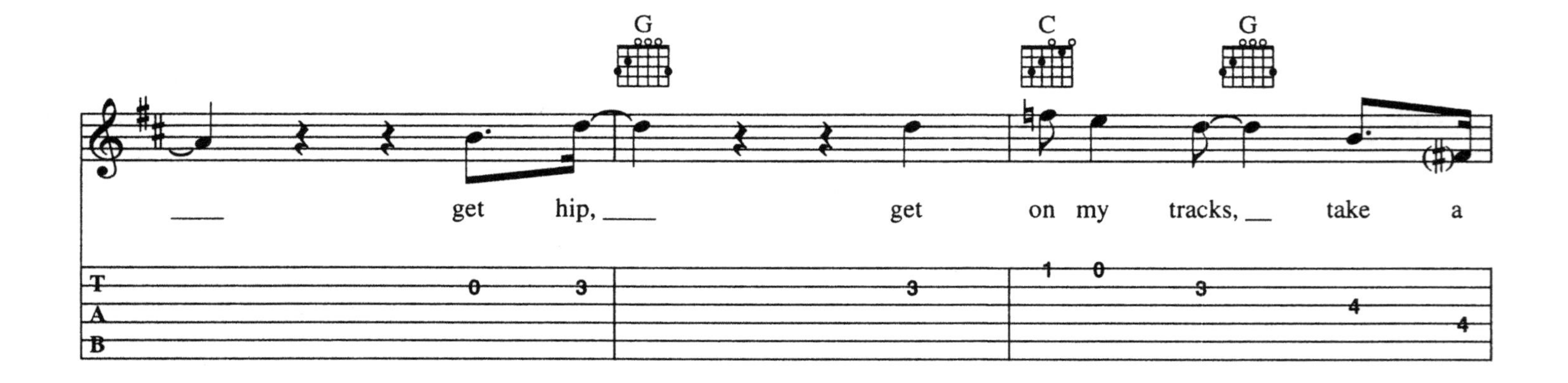
G
C
G
get hip, get on my tracks, take a

D
G
back seat, hitch - hike, and take a long ride on my

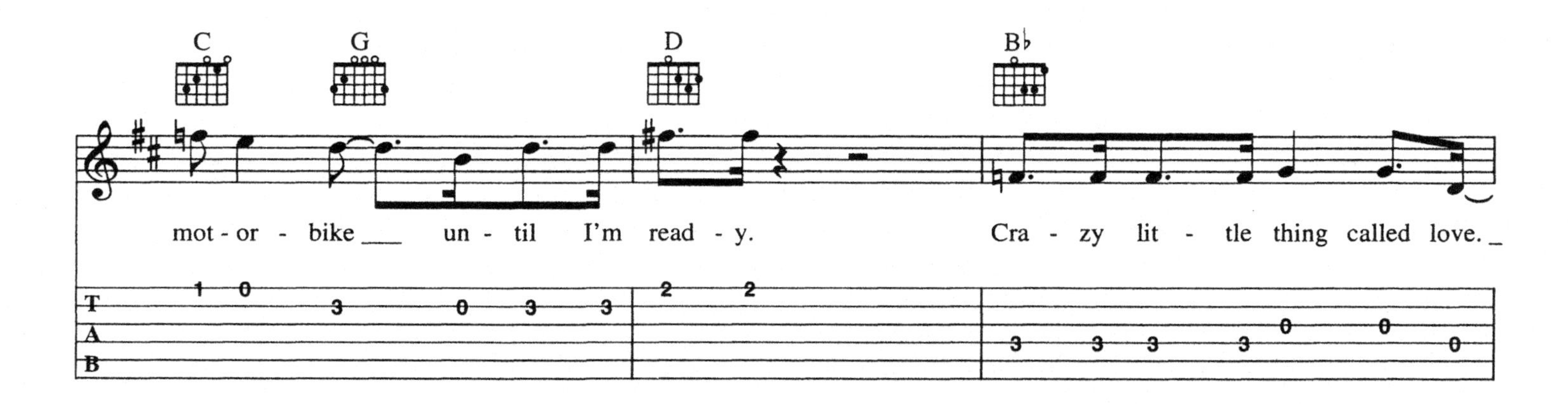
C
G
D
B♭
mot - or - bike until I'm read - y. Cra - zy lit - tle thing called love.

D
1.
2.
D. S. al Coda
There goes my
This thing

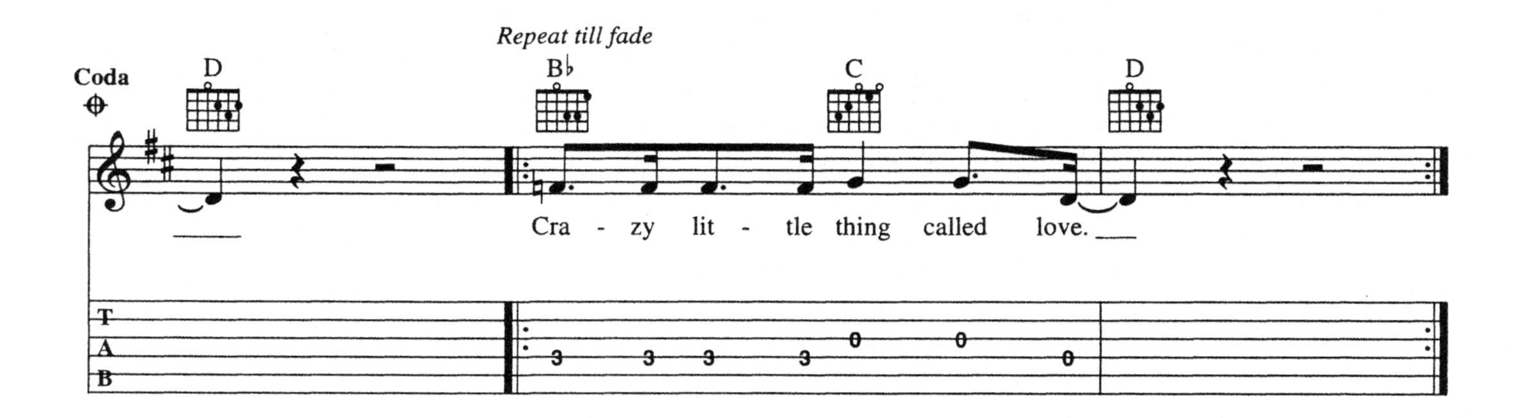
Repeat till fade
Coda
D
B♭
C
D
Cra - zy lit - tle thing called love.

# DON'T STOP ME NOW

Words and Music by FREDDIE MERCURY

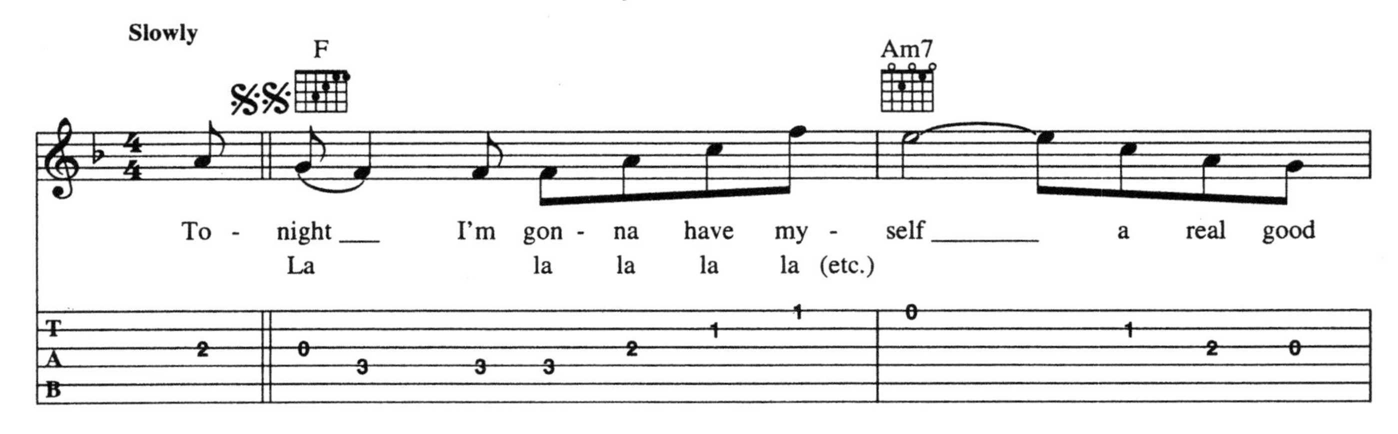


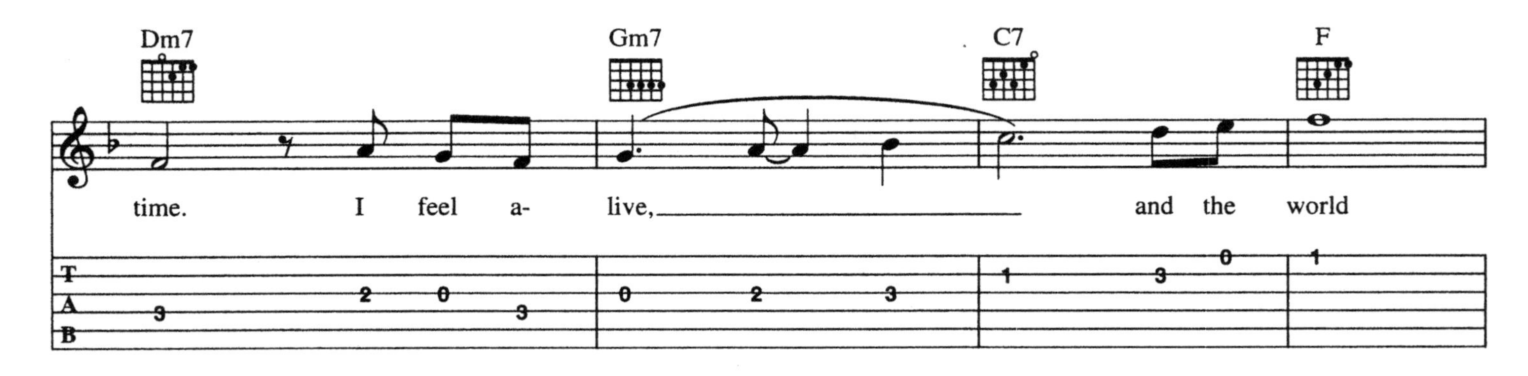


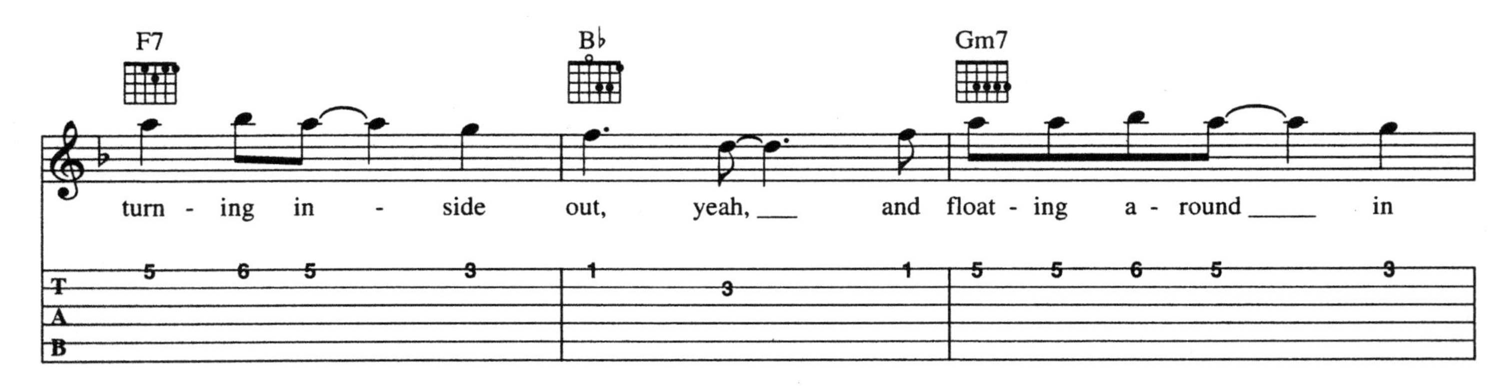

Brightly
C7
F
hav - in' a good __ time, hav - ing a good __ time. I'm a
1. shoot - ing star leap - ing through the
2. rock - et ship on my way to
3. Instrumental....
Am7
Dm7
Gm7
sky, like a ti - ger de - fy - ing the laws ____ of grav - i - ty. ___
Mars, on a col - li - sion course, I am a sat - el - lite, I'm
C7
F
Am
I'm a rac - ing car, pass - ing by like La - dy Go - di -
out of con - trol, I am a sex ma - chine read - y to re - load, like an
Dm
Gm7
C7
va. I'm gon - na go, go, ___ go. There's no stop - pin'
at - om bomb, a - bout to oh, oh, ___ oh, oh, oh, ex -
F
F7
B♭
me.
plode.
I'm burn - in' through ___ the sky, yeah. ____ Two

Gm7 D7 Gm
hun-dred de-grees, ___ that's why they call me Mis-ter Fahr- en - heit. ________ I'm
D7 Gm7 B♭
To Coda
trav-'ling at the speed of light. ____ I wan-na make a su-per-son-ic {man out / wom-an} of you. ___
C F Gm F Dm
___ Don't stop ___ me now, I'm hav - in' such a
Gm7 C7 F Gm F
good time, I'm hav - in' a ball. _____ Don't stop ___ me
Dm Gm7 D7
now, if you wan-na have a good time, just give me a call. ___________
T
A
B

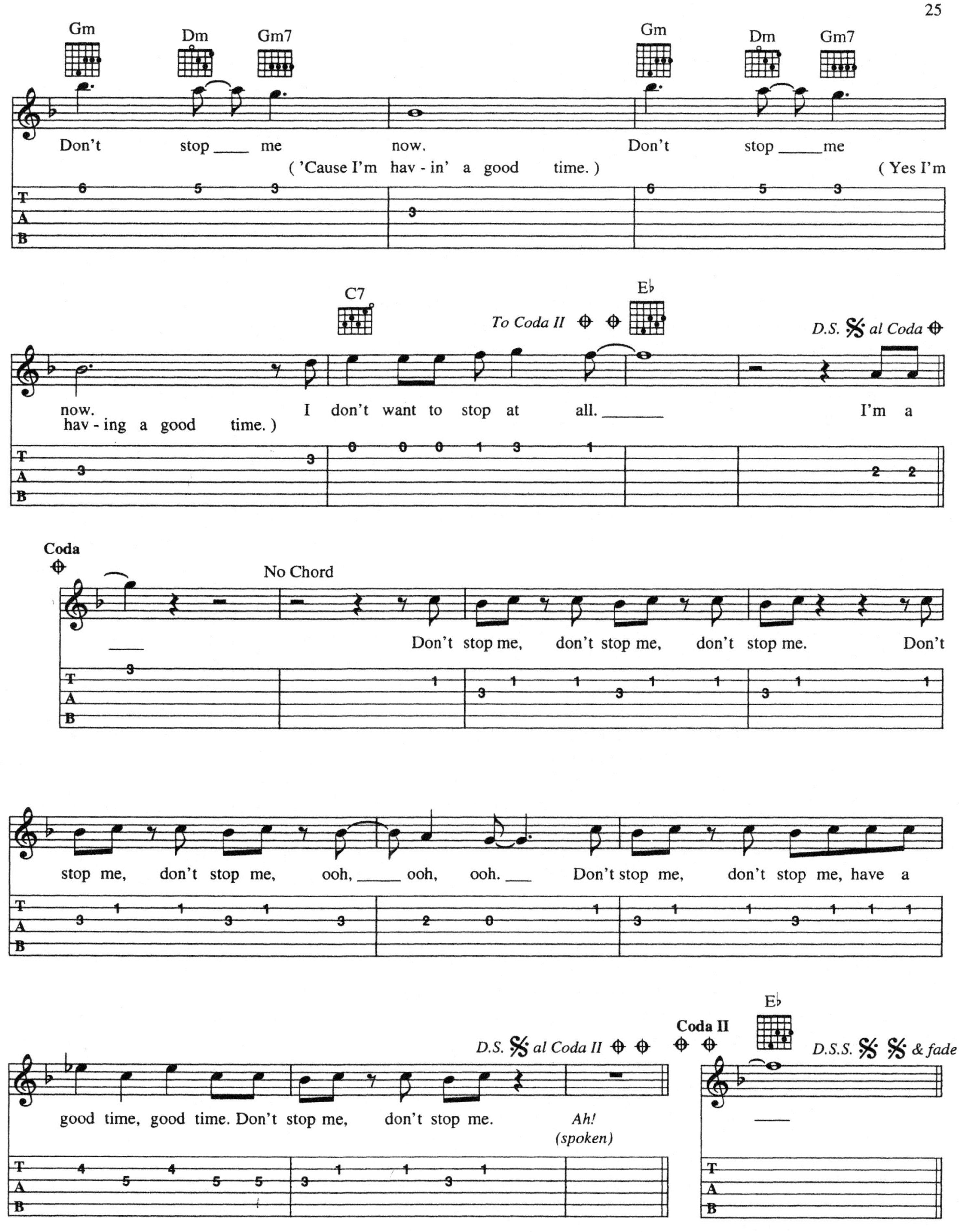
Gm
Dm
Gm7
Don't stop me now.
Don't stop me
('Cause I'm hav - in' a good time.)
(Yes I'm
now.
hav - ing a good time.)
C7
To Coda II
E♭
D.S. al Coda
I don't want to stop at all.
I'm a
Coda
No Chord
Don't stop me, don't stop me, don't stop me. Don't
stop me, don't stop me, ooh, ooh, ooh. Don't stop me, don't stop me, have a
good time, good time. Don't stop me, don't stop me.
Ah!
(spoken)
D.S. al Coda II
Coda II
D.S.S. & fade

# KILLER QUEEN

Words and Music by FREDDIE MERCURY

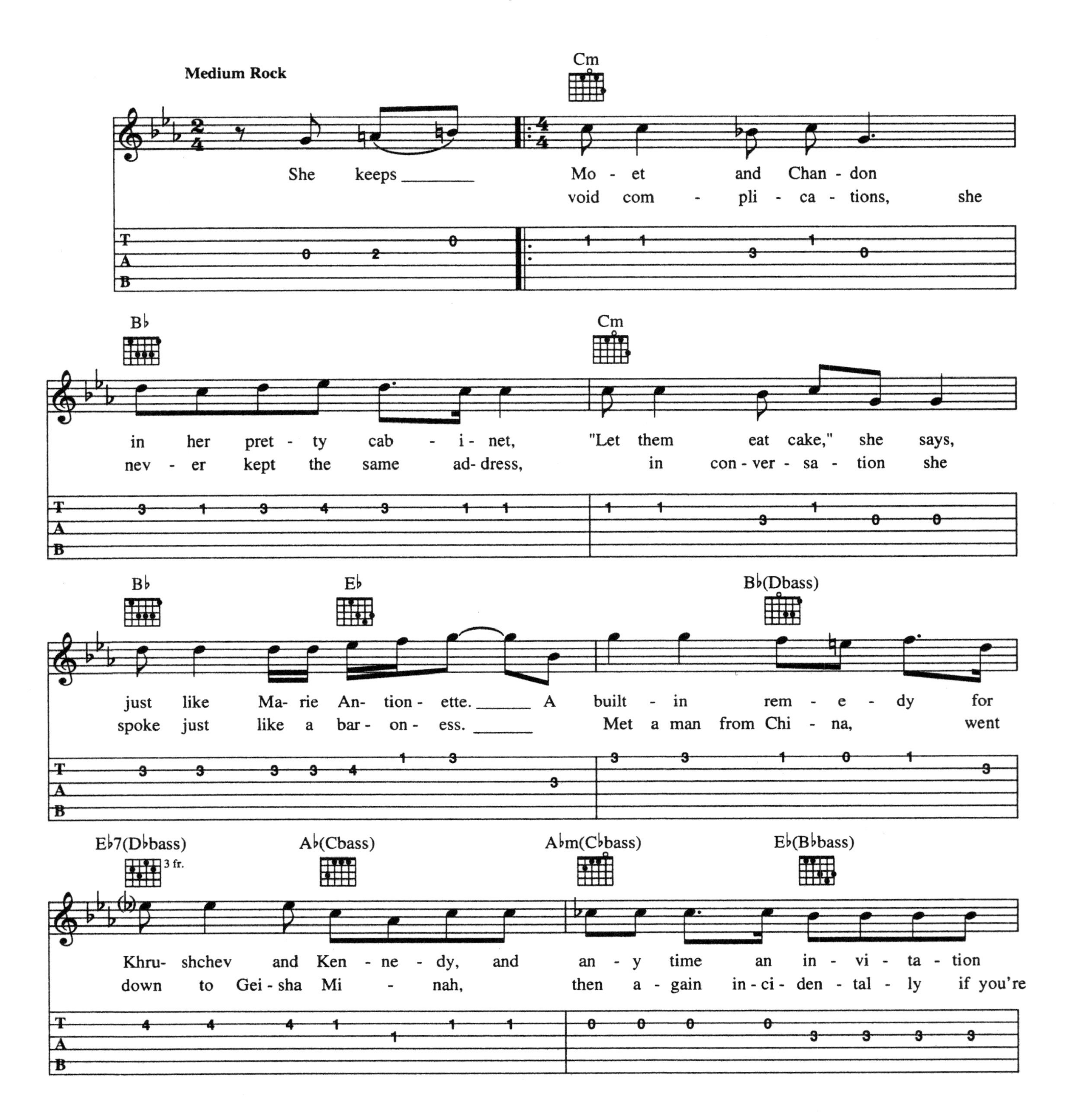

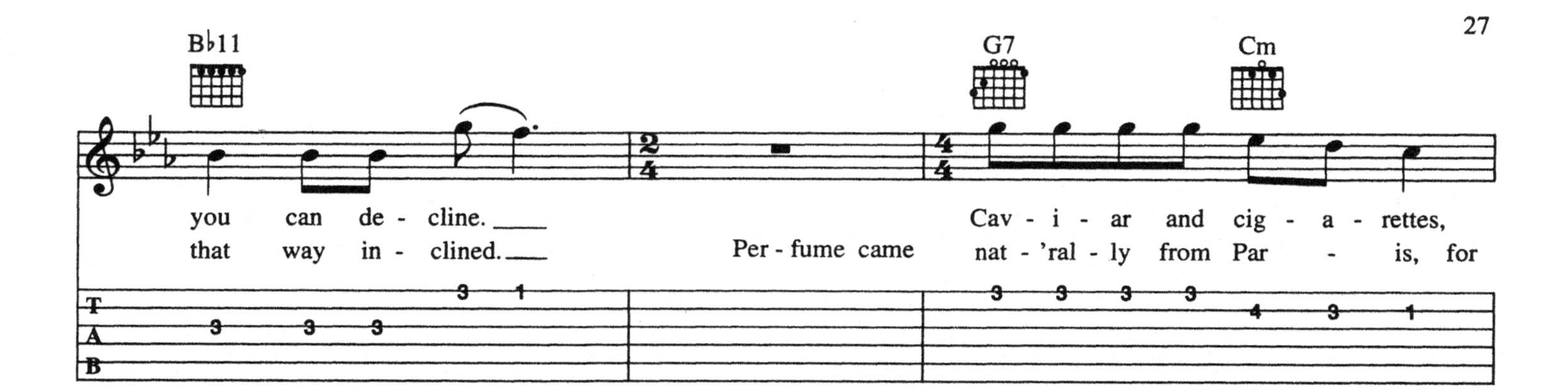
B♭11
G7
Cm
you can de - cline.
that way in - clined.
Per - fume came
Cav - i - ar and cig - a - rettes,
nat - 'ral - ly from Par - is, for
T
A
B

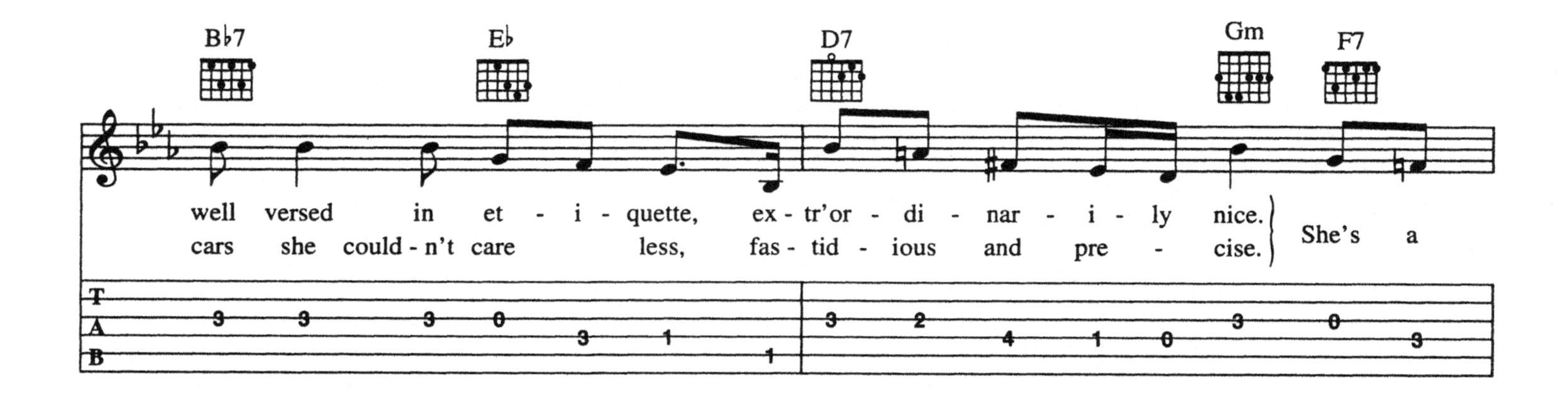
B♭7
E♭
D7
Gm
F7
well versed in et - i - quette, ex - tr'or - di - nar - i - ly nice.
cars she could - n't care less, fas - tid - ious and pre - cise.
She's a
T
A
B

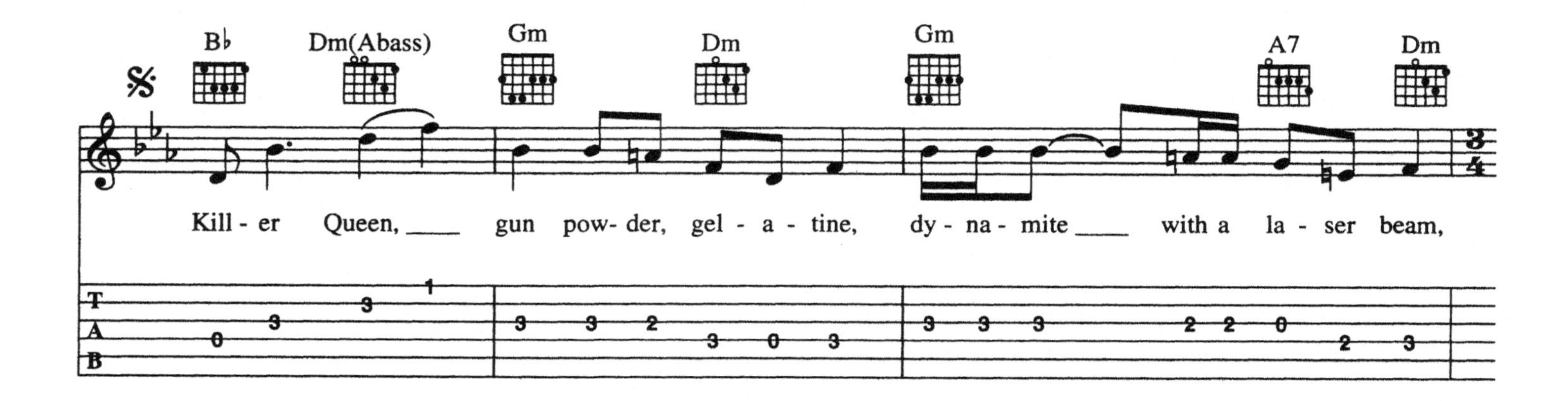
B♭
Dm(Abass)
Gm
Dm
Gm
A7
Dm
Kill - er Queen, gun pow - der, gel - a - tine, dy - na - mite with a la - ser beam,
T
A
B

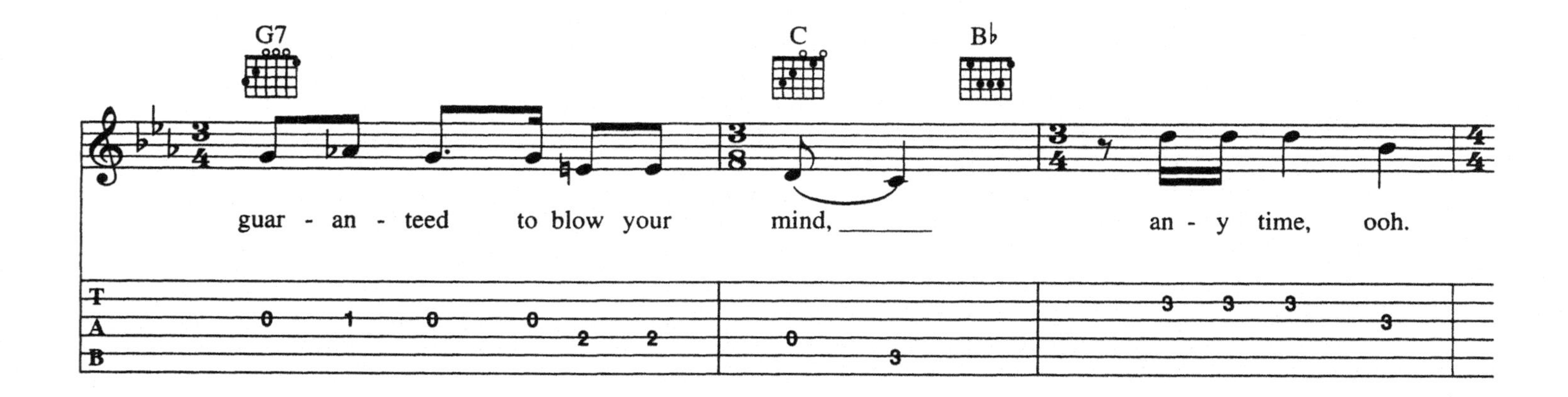
G7
C
B♭
guar - an - teed to blow your mind, an - y time, ooh.
T
A
B

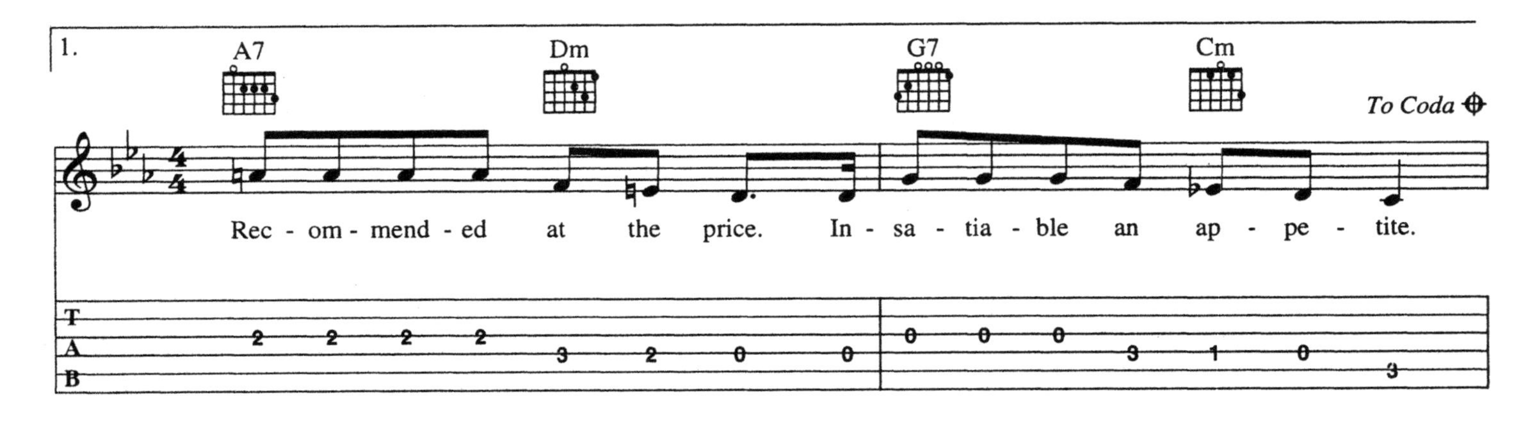
1.
A7
Dm
G7
Cm
To Coda
Rec - om - mend - ed at the price. In - sa - tia - ble an ap - pe - tite.

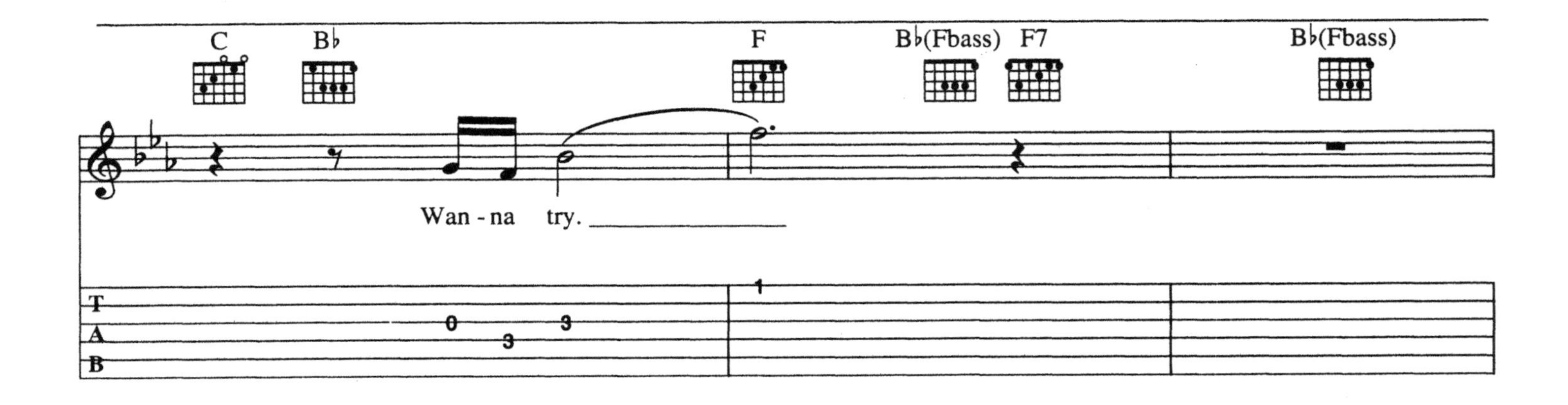
C
B♭
F
B♭(Fbass)
F7
B♭(Fbass)
Wan - na try.

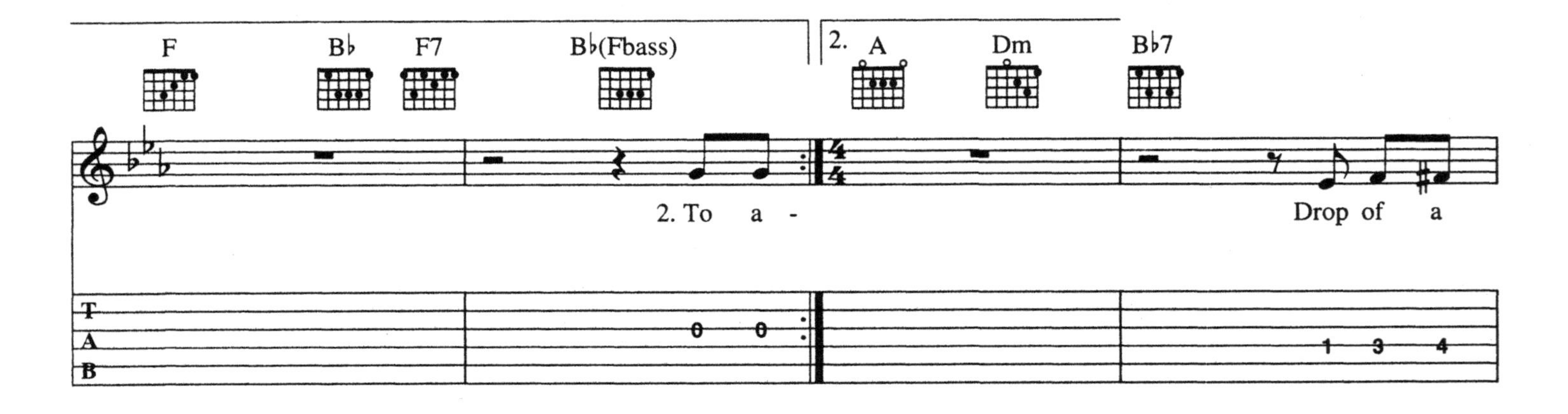
F
B♭
F7
B♭(Fbass)
2.
A
Dm
B♭7
2. To a -
Drop of a

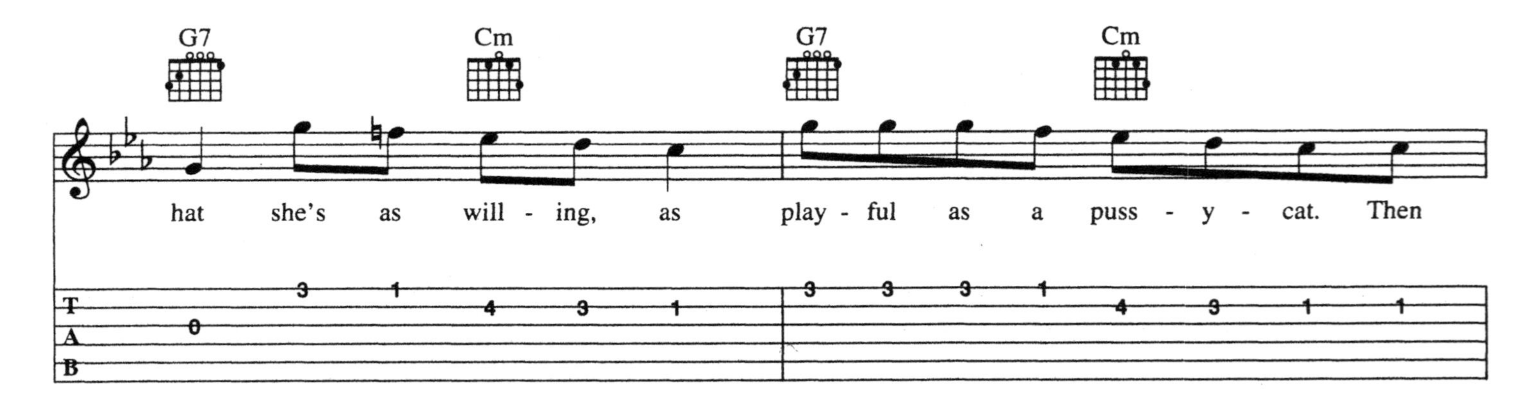
G7
Cm
G7
Cm
hat she's as will - ing, as play - ful as a puss - y - cat. Then

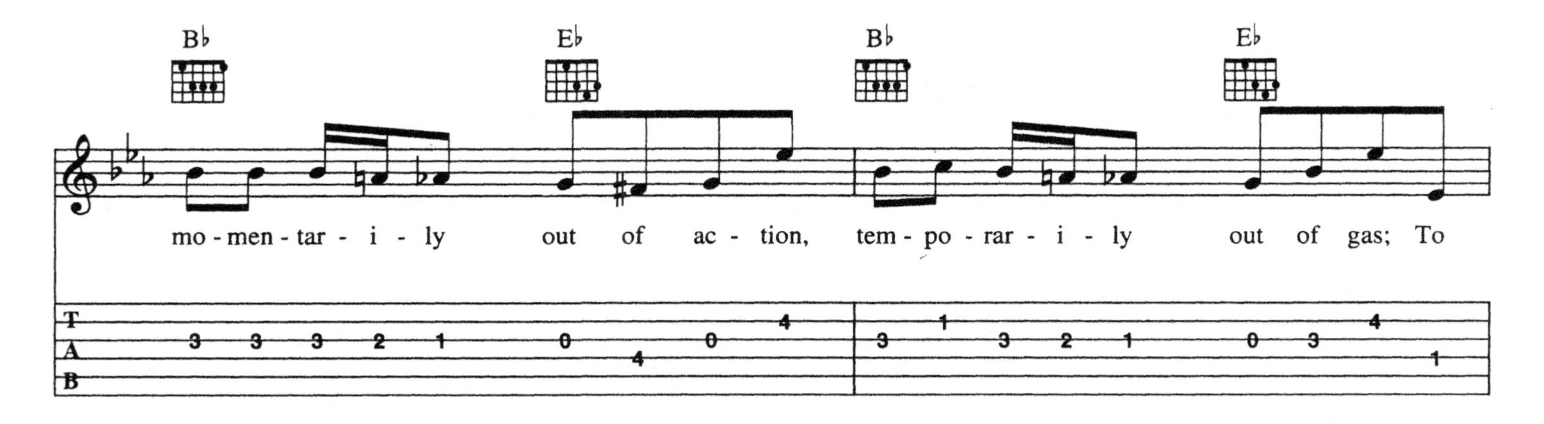
B♭
E♭
B♭
E♭
mo - men - tar - i - ly out of ac - tion, tem - po - rar - i - ly out of gas; To

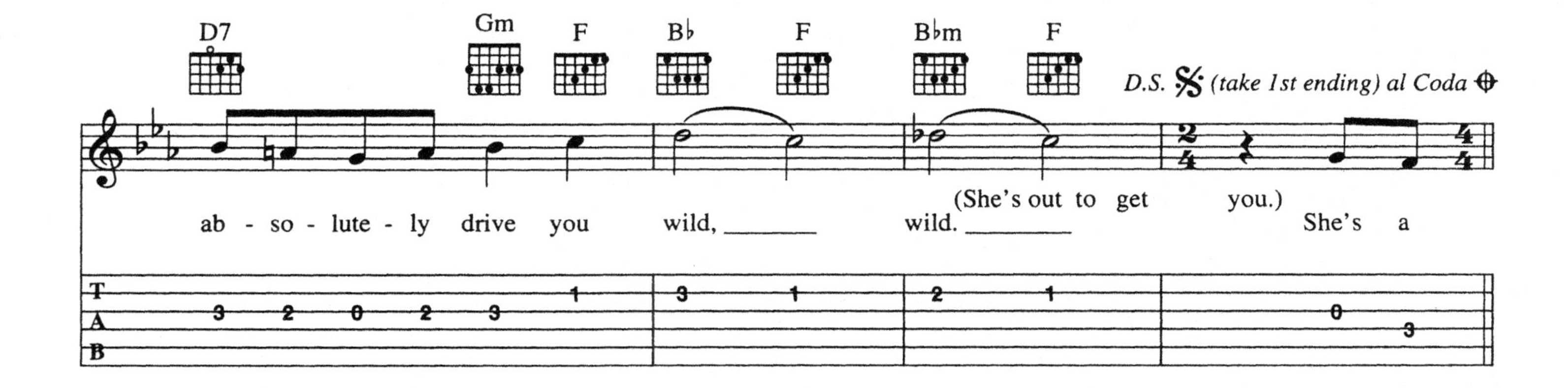
D7
Gm
F
B♭
F
B♭m
F
D.S. 𝄋 (take 1st ending) al Coda 𝄌
(She's out to get you.)
ab - so - lute - ly drive you wild, wild. She's a

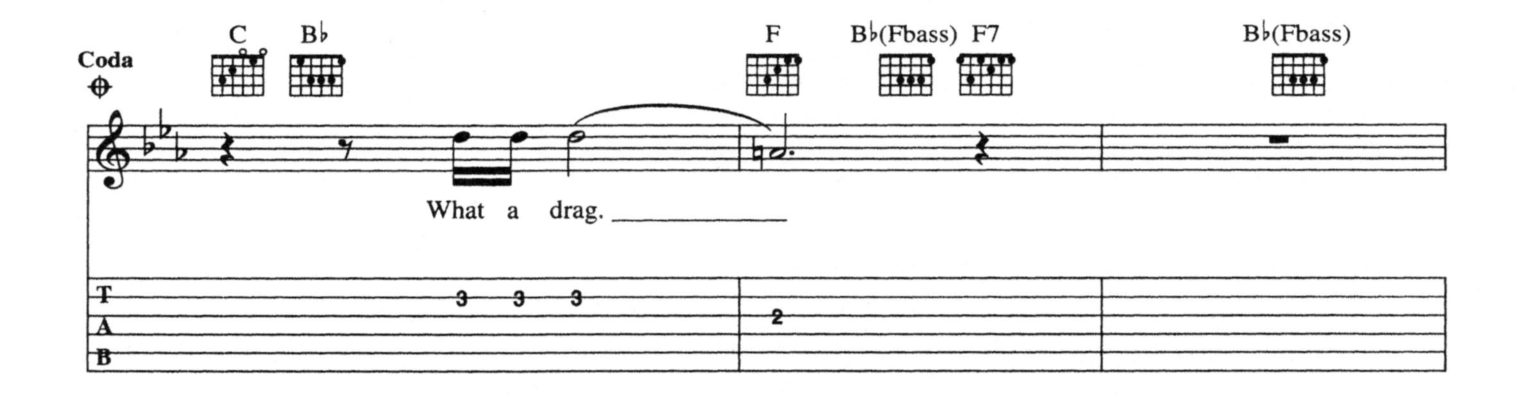
Coda
C
B♭
F
B♭(Fbass)
F7
B♭(Fbass)
What a drag.

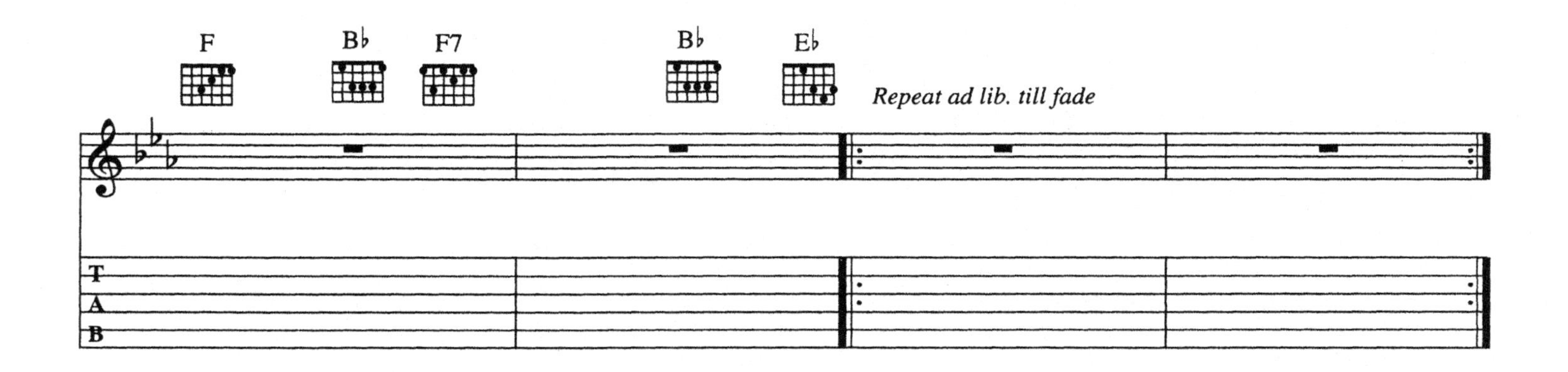
F
B♭
F7
B♭
E♭
Repeat ad lib. till fade

# NEED YOUR LOVING TONIGHT

Words and Music by
JOHN DEACON

B
E
C
E
I must be strong so she won't know _ how much I miss her.

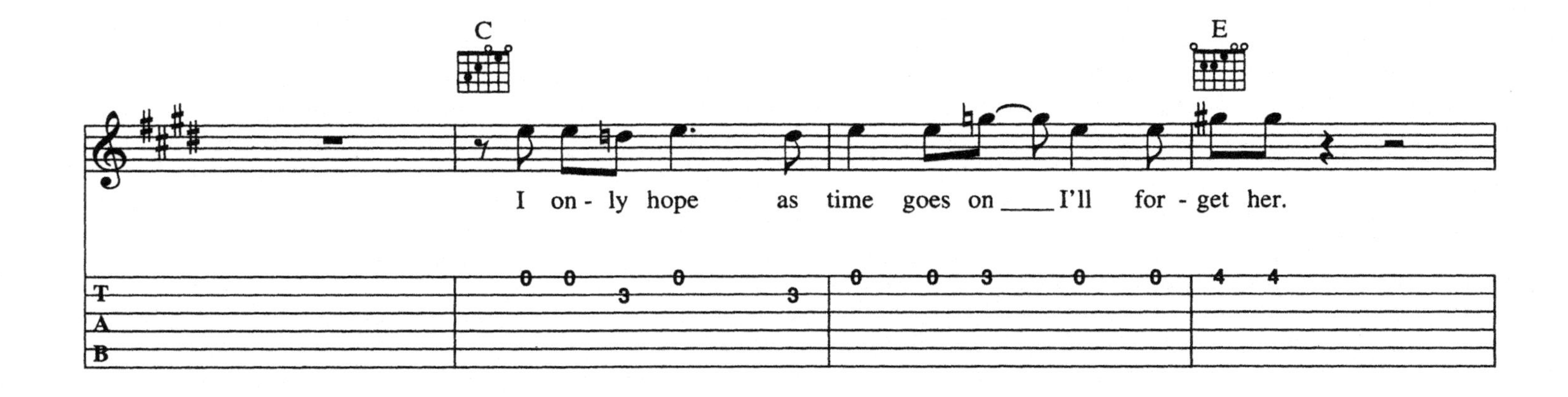
C
E
I on - ly hope as time goes on ____ I'll for - get her.

D
F♯
My bod - y's ach - ing, can't sleep at night, I'm too ex - haust- ed to

A
start a fight. ____ And if I see her with an - oth - er guy ____

B
E
I'll eat my heart out, 'cos I love her, love her, love her, love her. Come on ba- by, let's
T
A
B
2 2 2 4 0 0 0
4 0 4 0 4 0 4 0
0 0 0 0 2

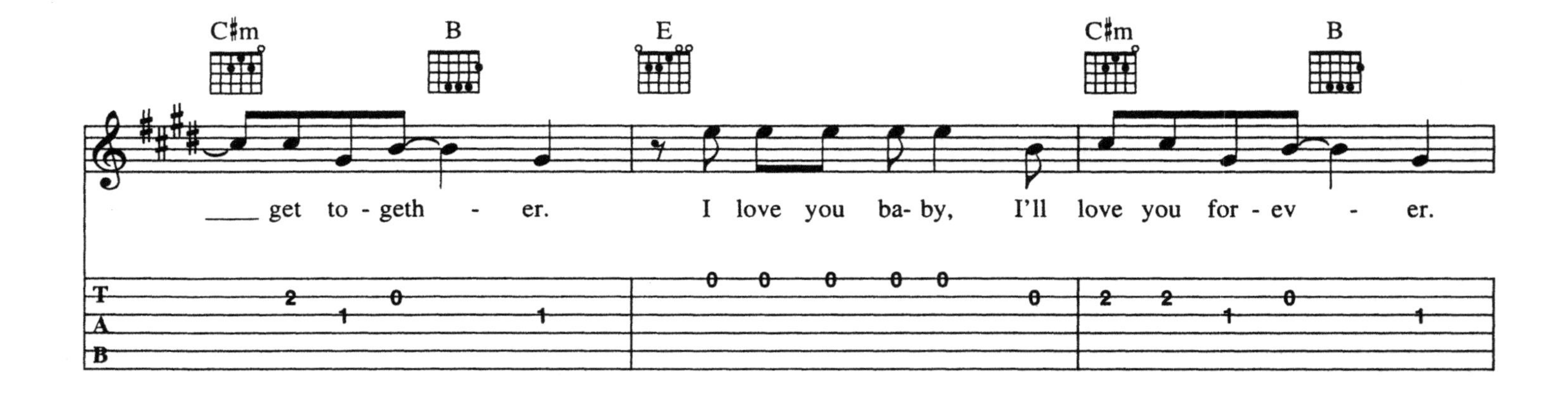
C♯m
B
E
C♯m
B
get to - geth - er. I love you ba- by, I'll love you for - ev - er.
T
A
B
2 1 0 1
0 0 0 0 0 0
2 2 1 0 1

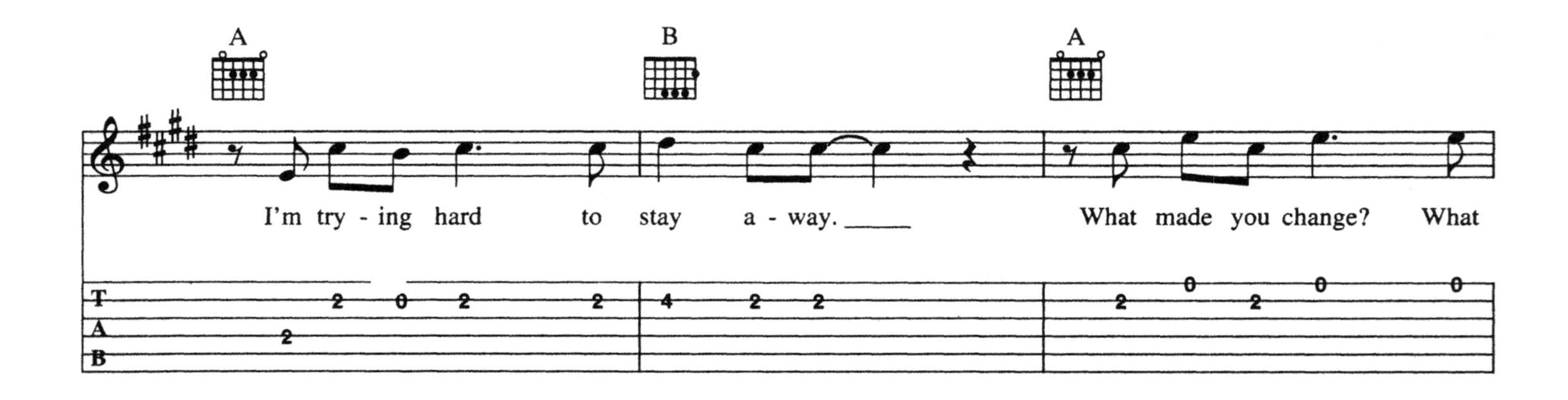
A
B
A
I'm try - ing hard to stay a - way. What made you change? What
T
A
B
2 2 0 2 2
4 2 2
2 0 2 0 0

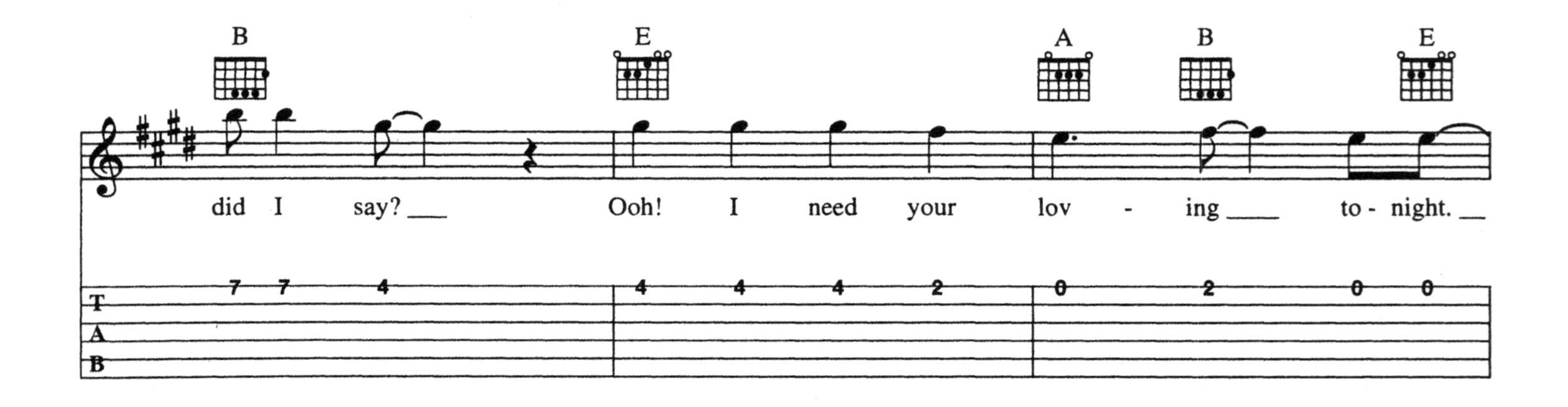
B
E
A
B
E
did I say? Ooh! I need your lov - ing to - night.
T
A
B
7 7 4
4 4 4 2
0 2 0 0

A
B
E
A
B
Ooh, I need your lov - ing.

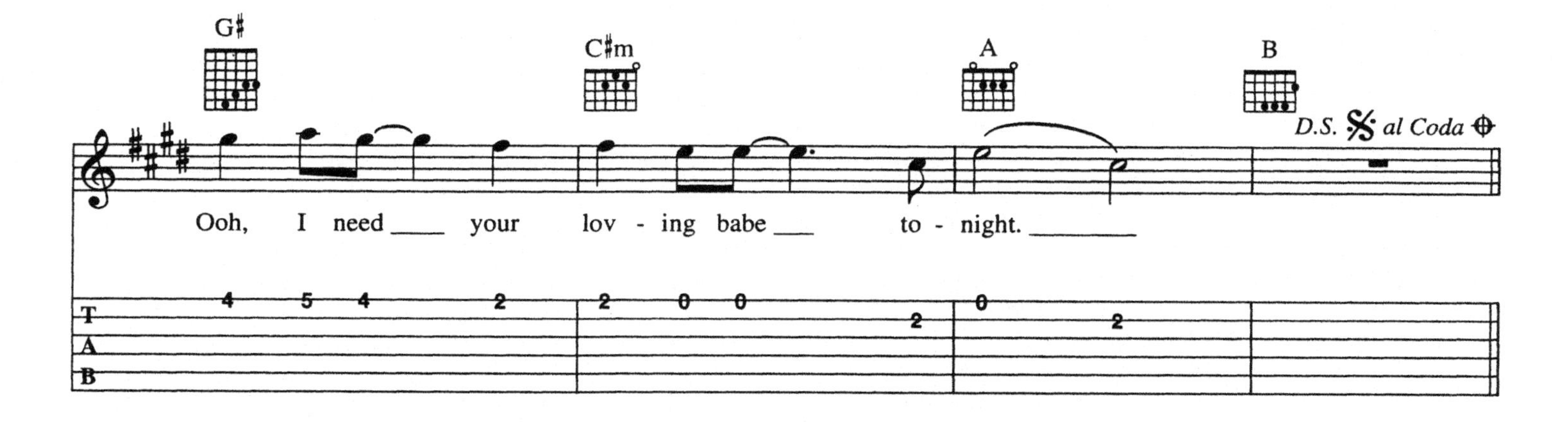
G♯
C♯m
A
B
D.S. al Coda
Ooh, I need your lov - ing babe to - night.

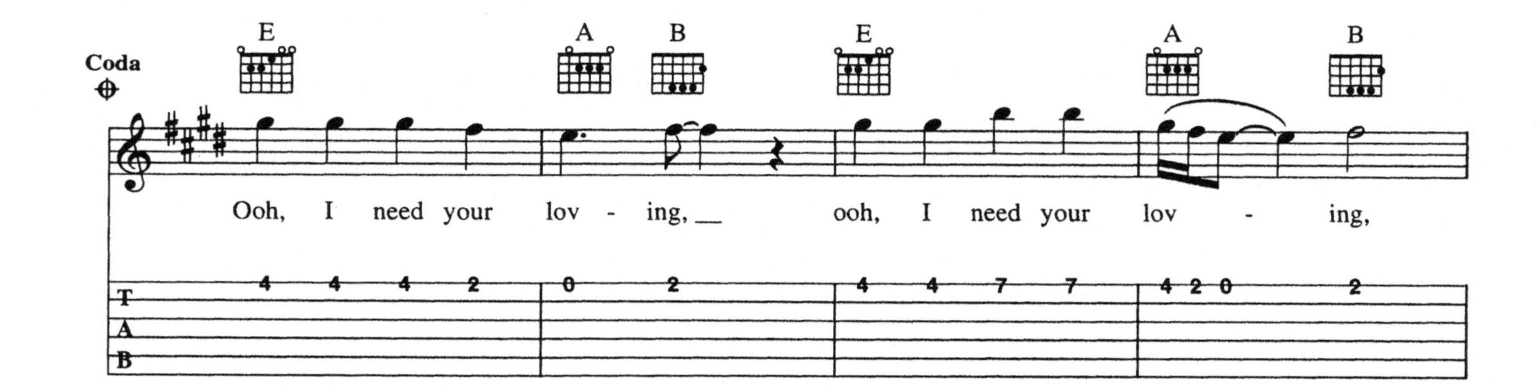
Coda
E
A
B
E
A
B
Ooh, I need your lov - ing, ooh, I need your lov - ing,

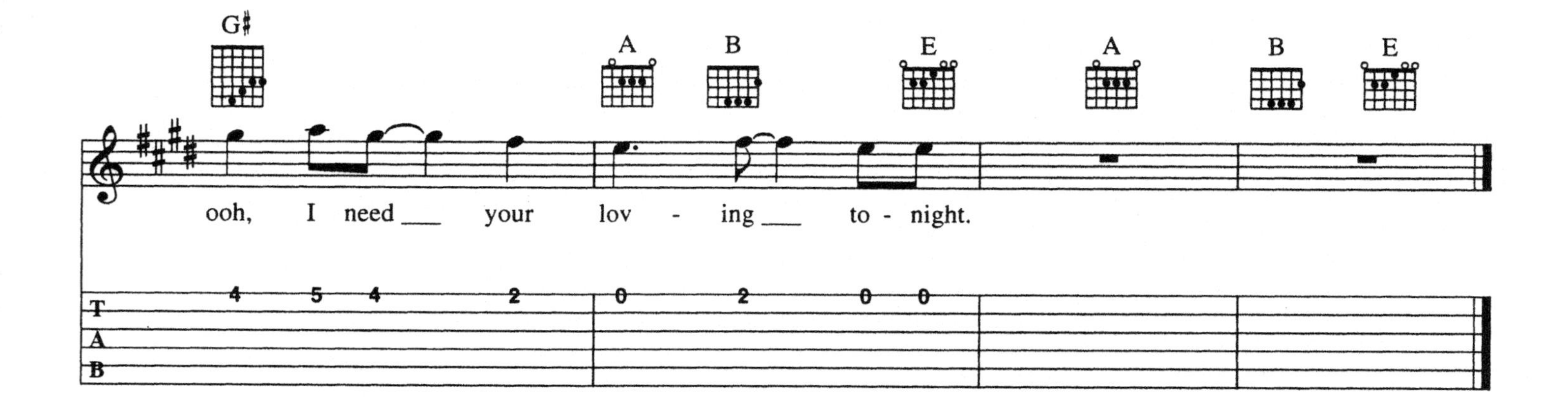
G♯
A
B
E
A
B
E
ooh, I need your lov - ing to - night.

# SOMEBODY TO LOVE

Words and Music by FREDDIE MERCURY

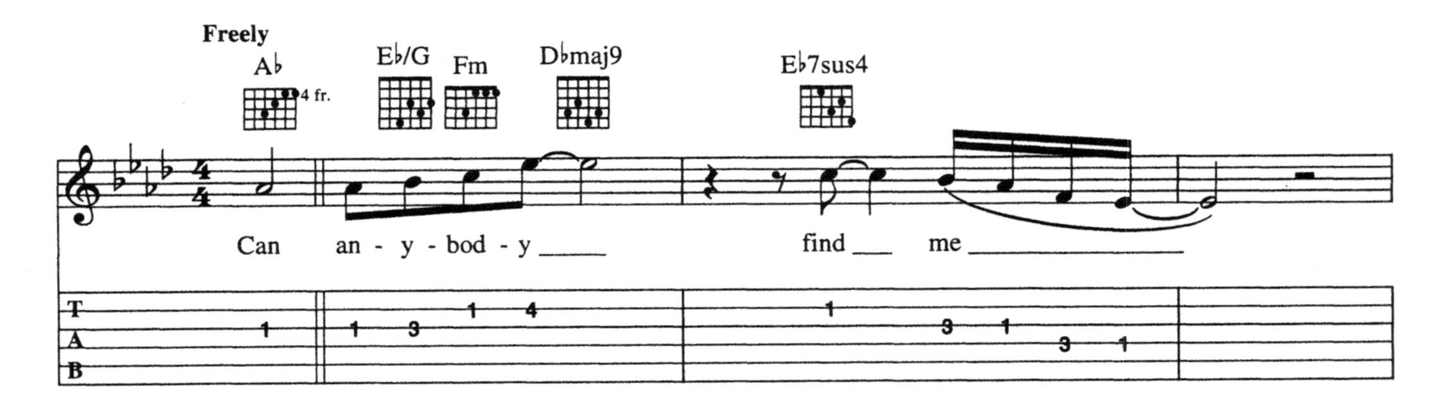


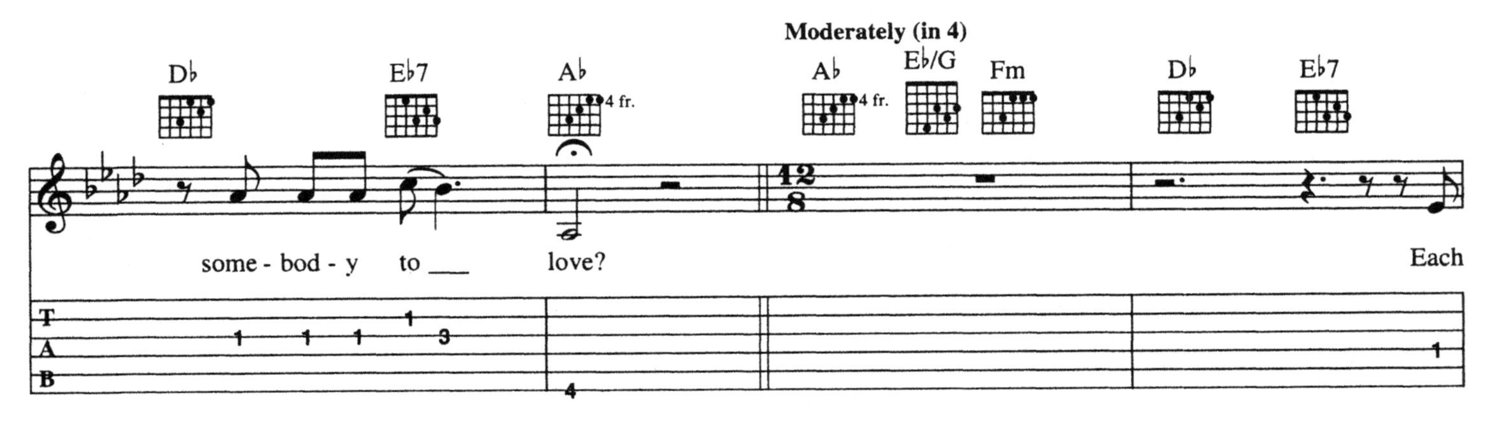

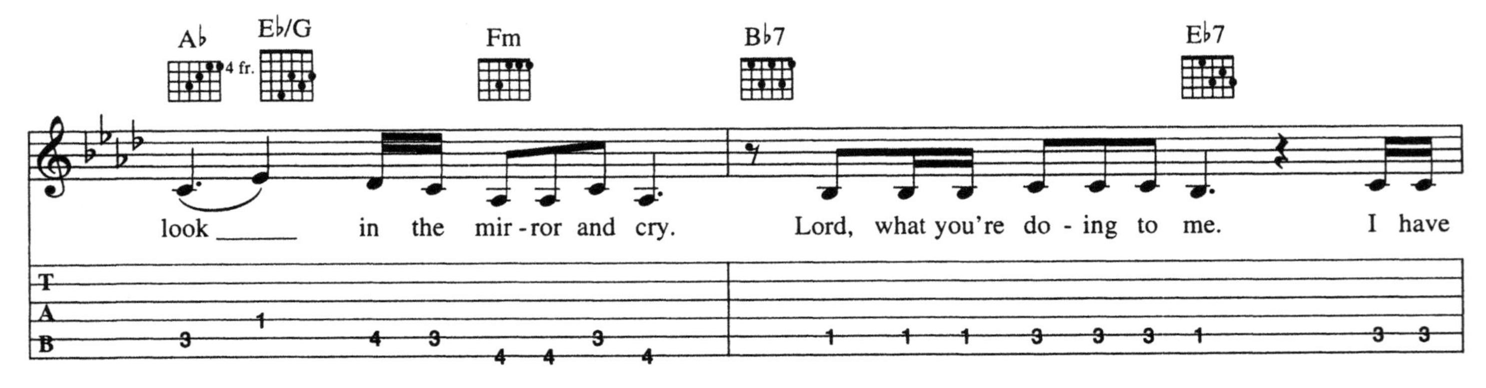

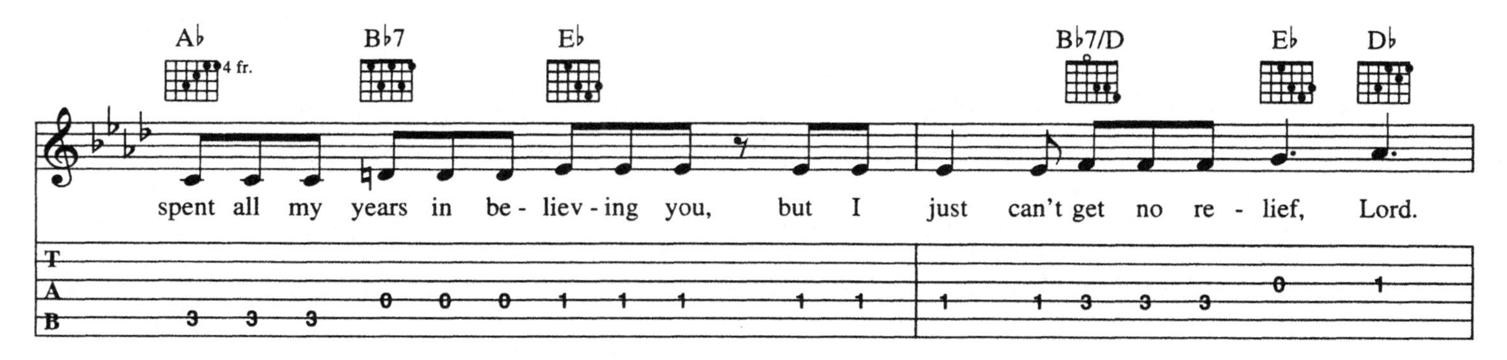
A♭ B♭7 E♭ B♭7/D E♭ D♭
spent all my years in be - liev - ing you, but I just can't get no re - lief, Lord.

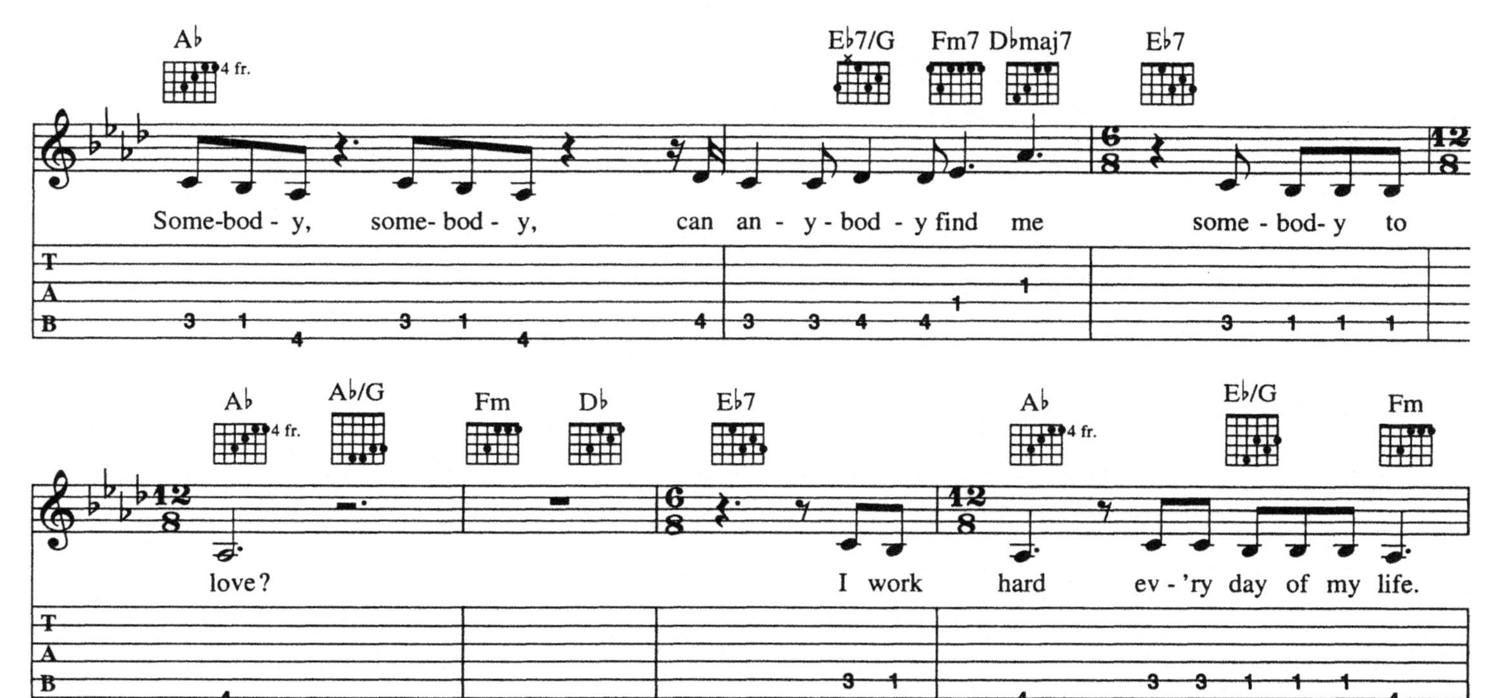
A♭ E♭7/G Fm7 D♭maj7 E♭7
Some-bod - y, some- bod - y, can an - y - bod - y find me some - bod- y to
A♭ A♭/G Fm D♭ E♭7 A♭ E♭/G Fm
love? I work hard ev - 'ry day of my life.

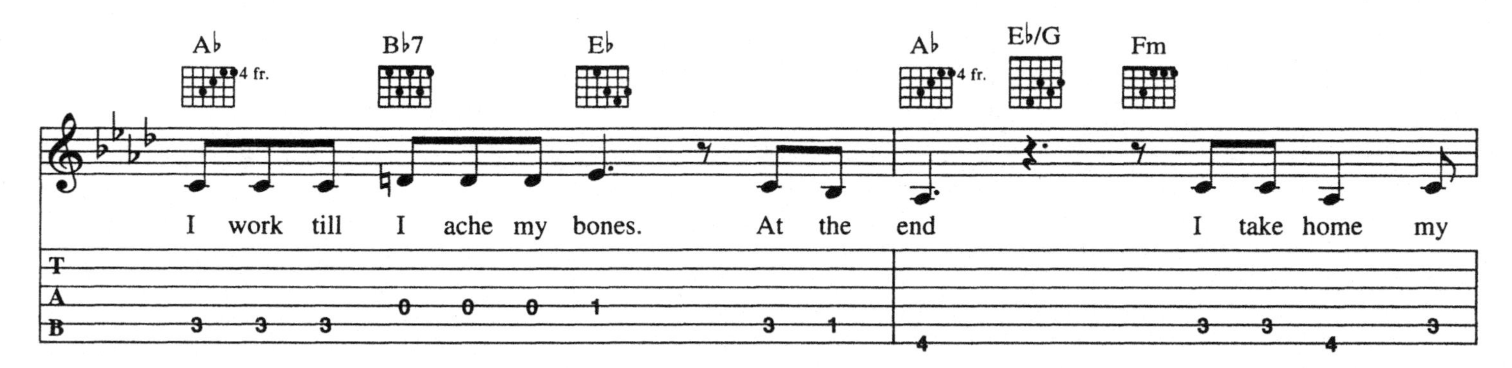
A♭ B♭7 E♭ A♭ E♭/G Fm
I work till I ache my bones. At the end I take home my

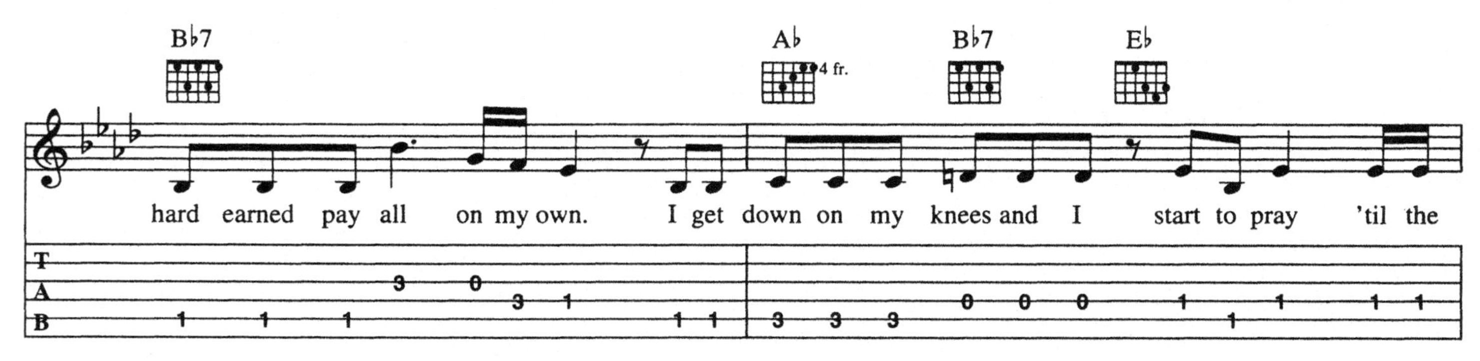
B♭7 A♭ B♭7 E♭
hard earned pay all on my own. I get down on my knees and I start to pray 'til the

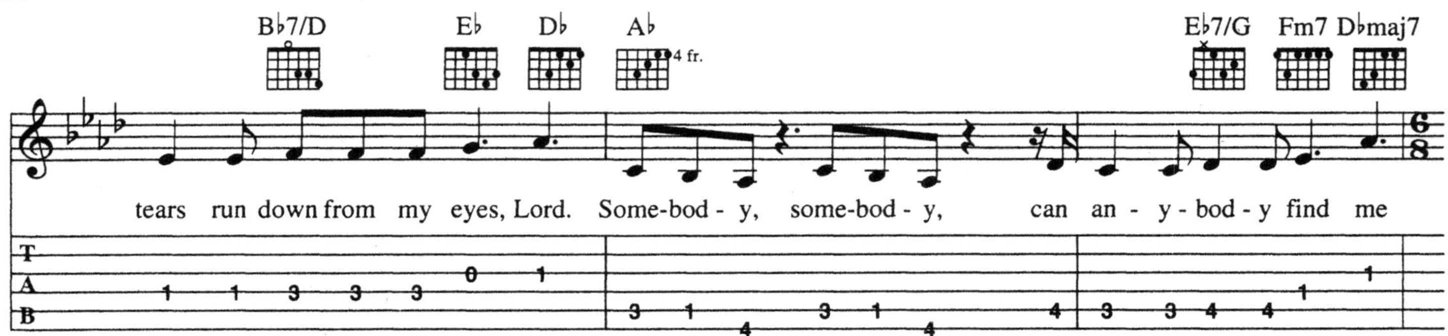
B♭7/D E♭ D♭ A♭ E♭7/G Fm7 D♭maj7
4 fr.
tears run down from my eyes, Lord. Some-bod - y, some-bod - y, can an - y - bod - y find me

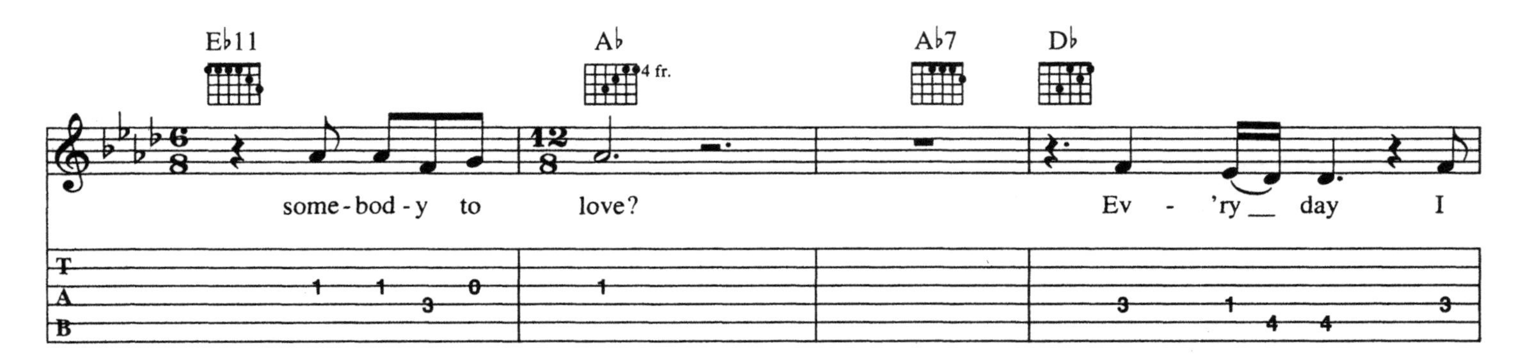
E♭11 A♭ A♭7 D♭
4 fr.
some-bod - y to love? Ev - 'ry day I

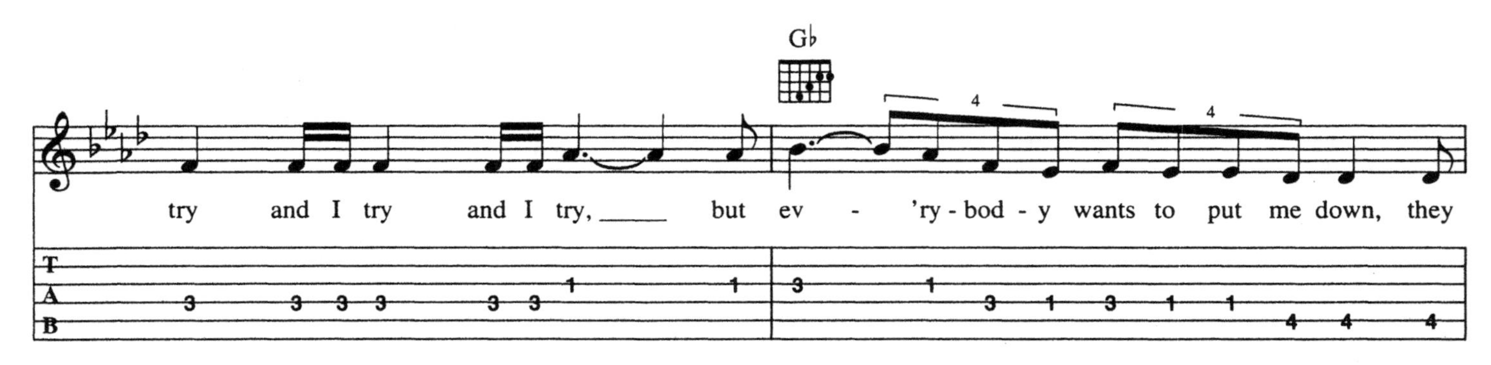
G♭
try and I try and I try, but ev - 'ry-bod - y wants to put me down, they

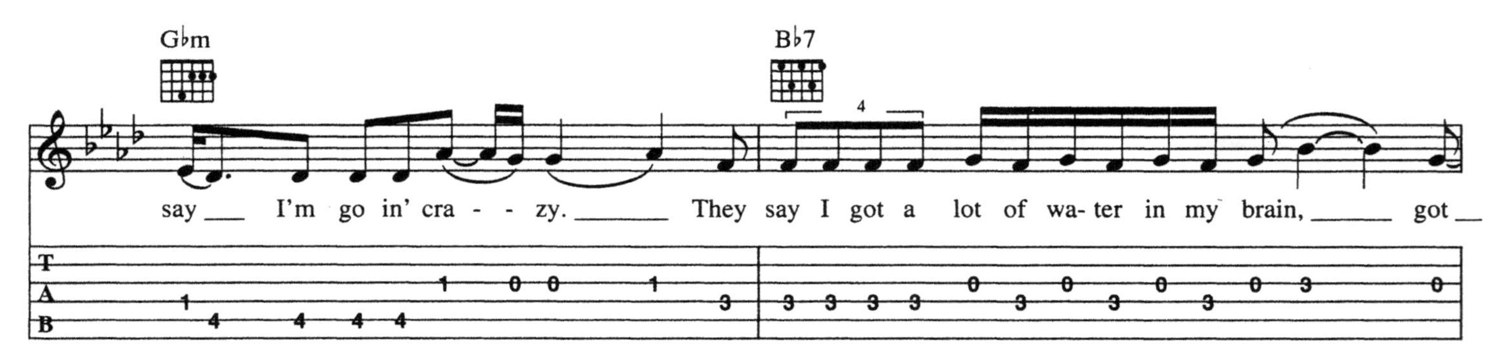
G♭m B♭7
say I'm go in' cra - - zy. They say I got a lot of wa- ter in my brain, got

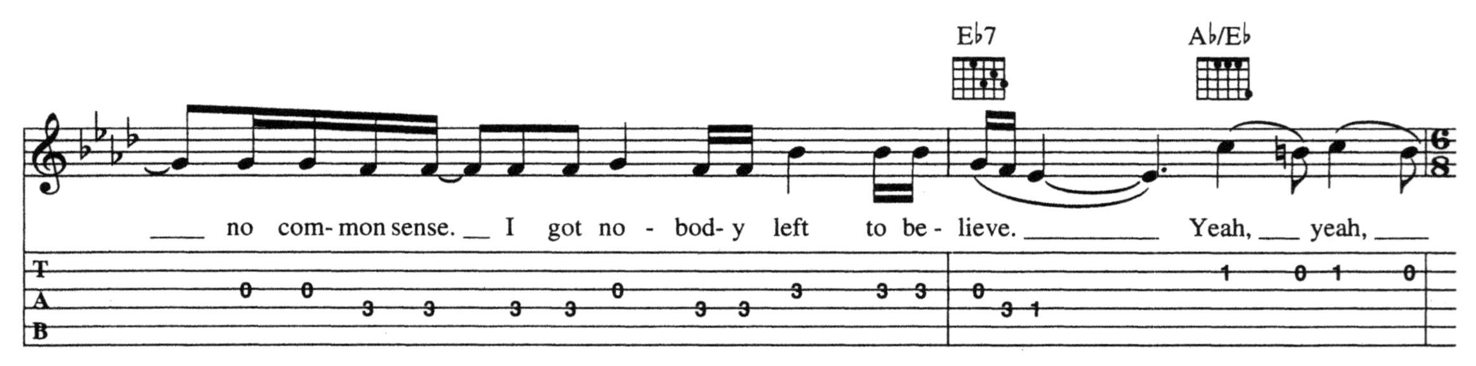
E♭7 A♭/E♭
no com- mon sense. I got no - bod- y left to be- lieve. Yeah, yeah,

A♭
E♭7/G
Fm7
D♭maj7
yeah, ____ yeah. ____ Ooh, some - bod - y, some - bod - y, can an - y - bod - y find me
E♭7
A♭
A♭/G
Fm
D♭maj7
E♭7
some - bod - y to love? ____ Got no
A♭
E♭7/G
Fm
A♭
B♭7
E♭7
feel, ____ I got no rhy - thm, I ______ just keep los - ing my beat. _____ I'm
A♭
E♭/G
Fm
B♭7
E♭7
O. K., I'm al - right, ain't gon - na face ______ no de - feat. I just
A♭
B♭7
E♭
B♭7/D
E♭
D♭
got - ta get out of this pris - on cell, __ one day I'm gon - na be free, Lord. ______

No Chord
Find me some - bod - y to love, find me some - bod - y to love,
A♭
4 fr.
find me some - bod - y to love, find me some - bod - y to love,

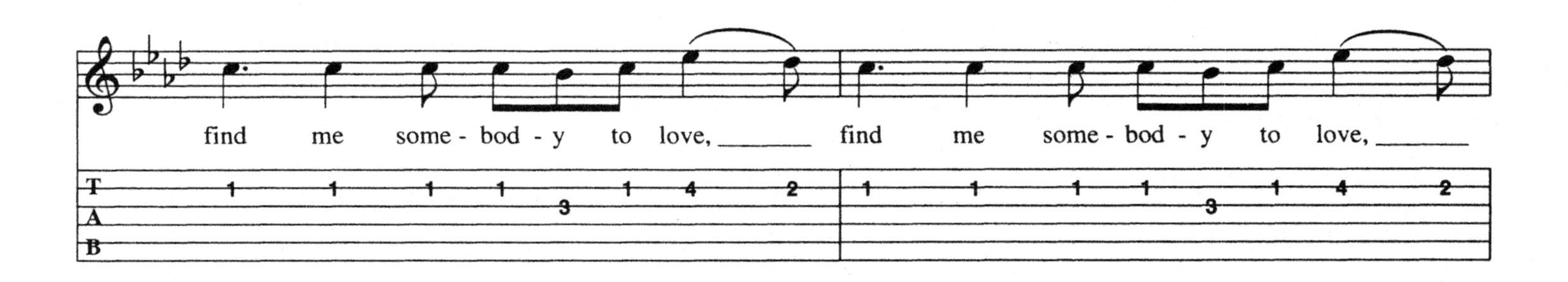
find me some - bod - y to love, find me some - bod - y to love,

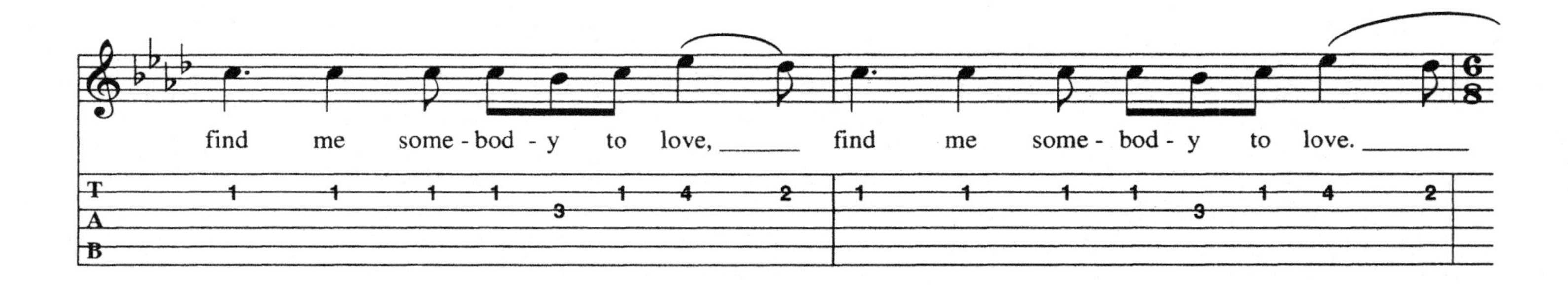
find me some - bod - y to love, find me some - bod - y to love.

Find me some - bod - y to love,

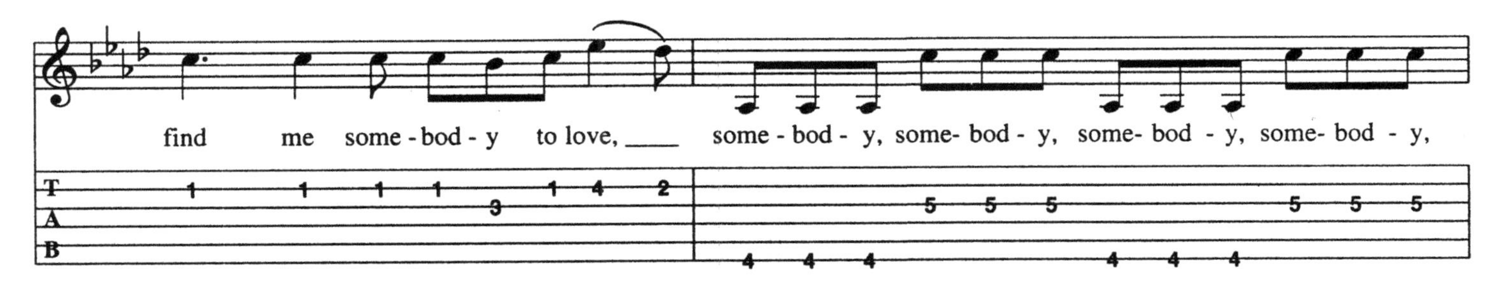
find me some-bod-y to love,
some-bod-y, some-bod-y, some-bod-y, some-bod-y,

E♭ D♭ A♭
4 fr.
E♭7/G Fm7 D♭maj7
some-bod-y. Find me some-bod-y, find me some - bod-y to love. Can an-y-bod-y find me

Freely
N.C.
some-bod-y to love?

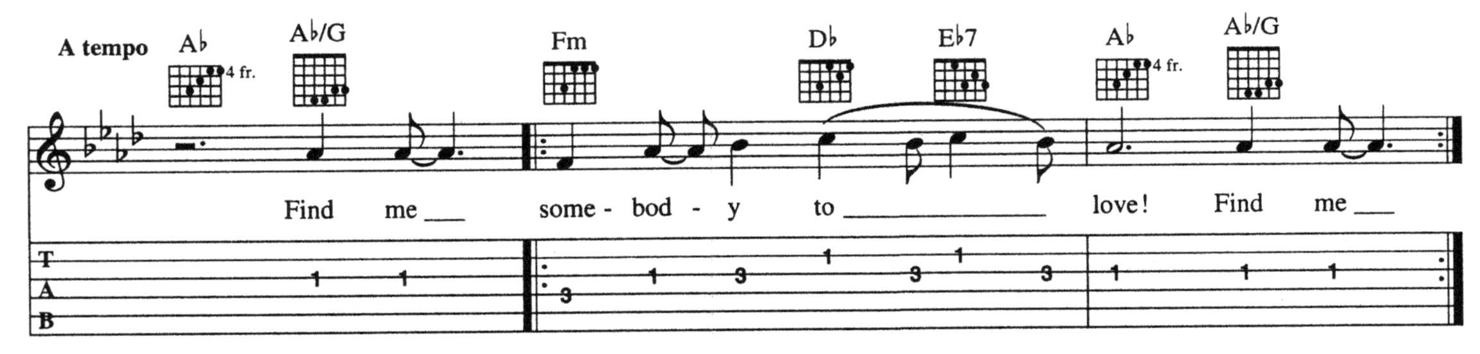
A tempo
A♭ A♭/G Fm D♭ E♭7 A♭ A♭/G
4 fr.
Find me some-bod-y to love! Find me

Fm D♭ E♭7 A♭
4 fr.
some-bod-y to love! Find me, find me, find me, find me.

# ANOTHER ONE BITES THE DUST

Words and Music by
JOHN DEACON

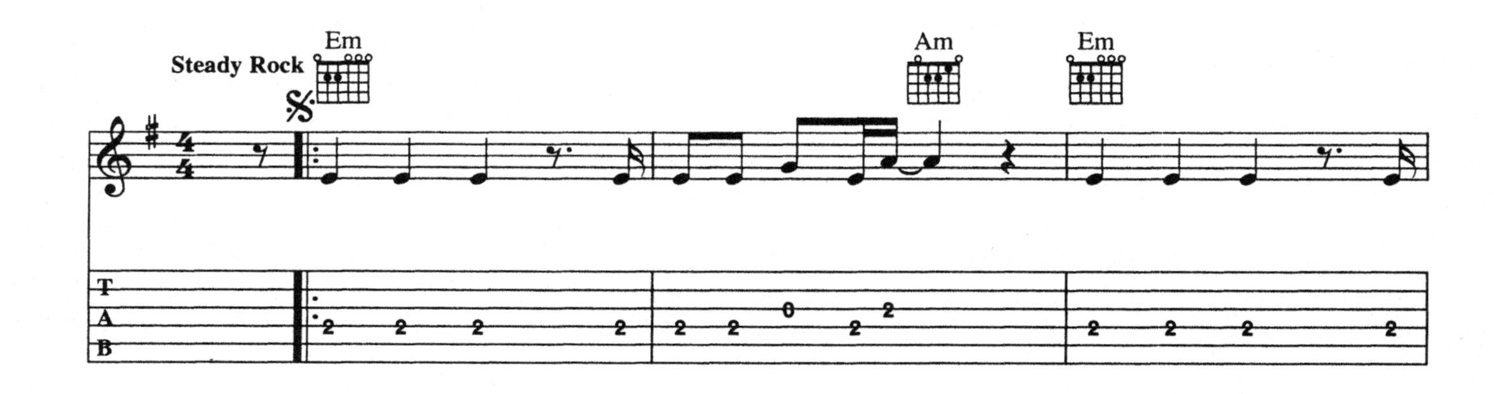
Steady Rock
Em
Am
Em
T
A
B

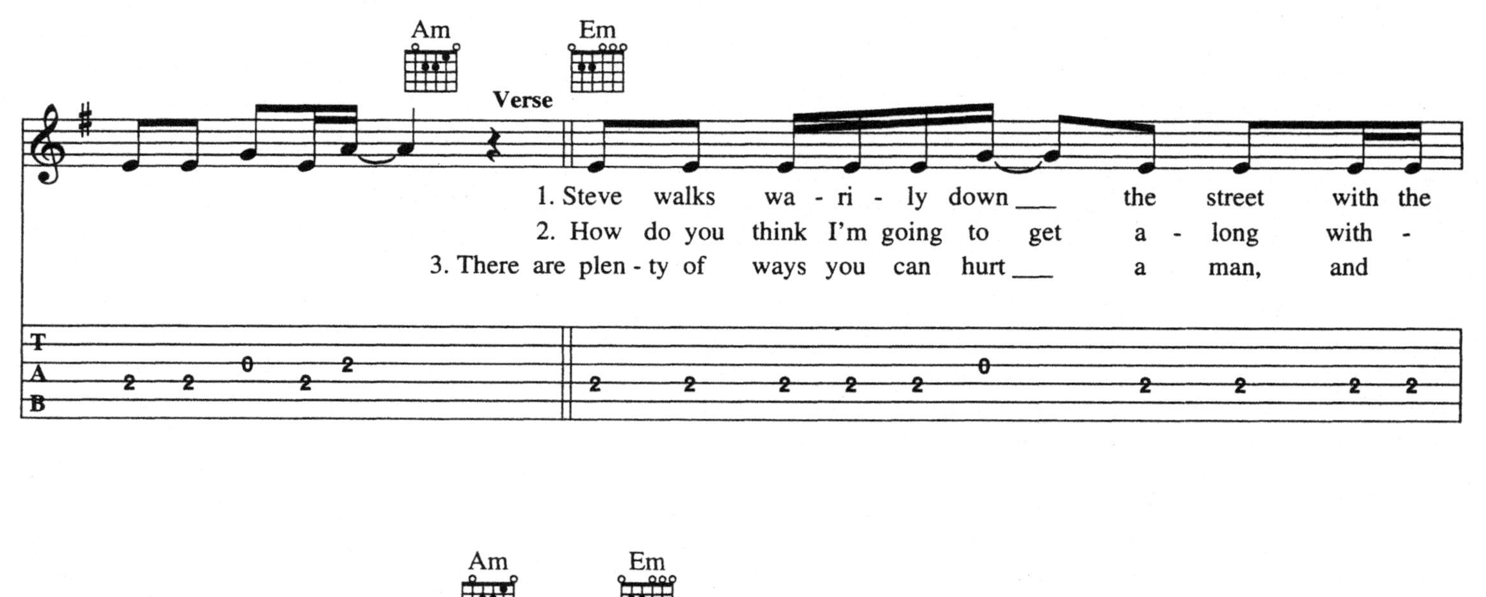
Am
Em
Verse
1. Steve walks wa - ri - ly down ___ the street with the
2. How do you think I'm going to get a - long with -
3. There are plen - ty of ways you can hurt ___ a man, and
T
A
B

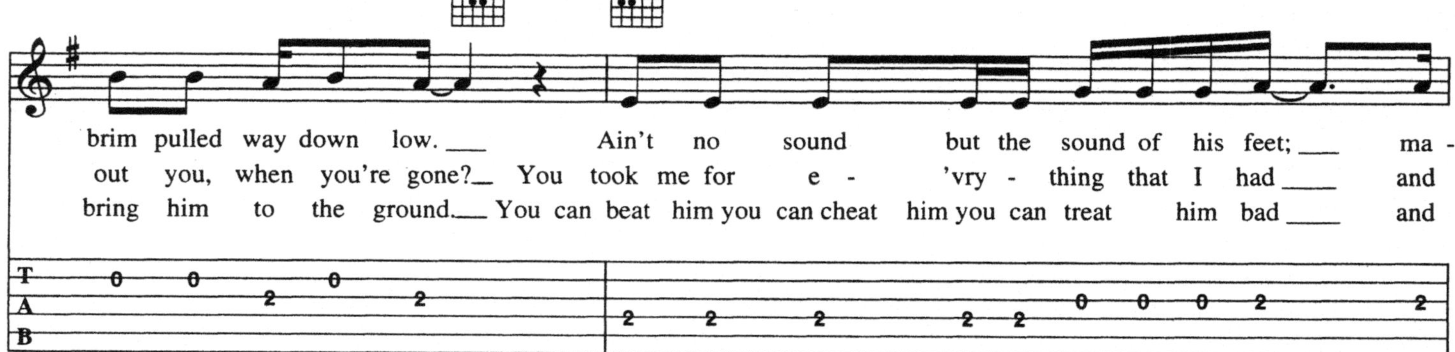
Am
Em
brim pulled way down low. ___ Ain't no sound but the sound of his feet; ___ ma -
out you, when you're gone?__ You took me for e - 'vry - thing that I had ___ and
bring him to the ground.__ You can beat him you can cheat him you can treat him bad ___ and
T
A
B

Am
C
G
chine guns rea - dy to go.
Are you rea - dy, hey!
Are you rea - dy for this?
Are you
kicked me out on my own.
Are you hap - py?
Are you sa - tis - fied?
How
leave him when he's down.
But I'm rea - dy,
yes I'm rea - dy for you.
I'm
hang - ing on the edge of your seat?
Out of the door - way the bul - lets rip
long can you stand the heat?
Out of the door - way the bul - lets rip
stand - ing on my own two feet.
Out of the door - way the bul - lets rip, re -
B
Em
Chorus
to the sound of the beat.
to the sound of the beat.
peat - ing the sound of the beat.
An - oth - er one bites the dust.
An - oth - er one bites the dust.
And an -

Em
Am
oth - er one gone and an - oth - er one gone. An - oth - er One Bites The Dust.
F♯m
To Coda
1.
B
Hey! I'm gon - na get you too. An - oth - er one bites the dust.
2.
B
No Chord
oth - er one bites the dust. An - oth - er one bites the dust. An -
oth - er one bites the dust. An - oth - er one bites the dust. An -
D. S. al Coda
oth - er one bites the dust.
Coda
F♯m
B
oth - er one bites the dust.

# BRIGHTON ROCK

Words and Music by BRIAN MAY

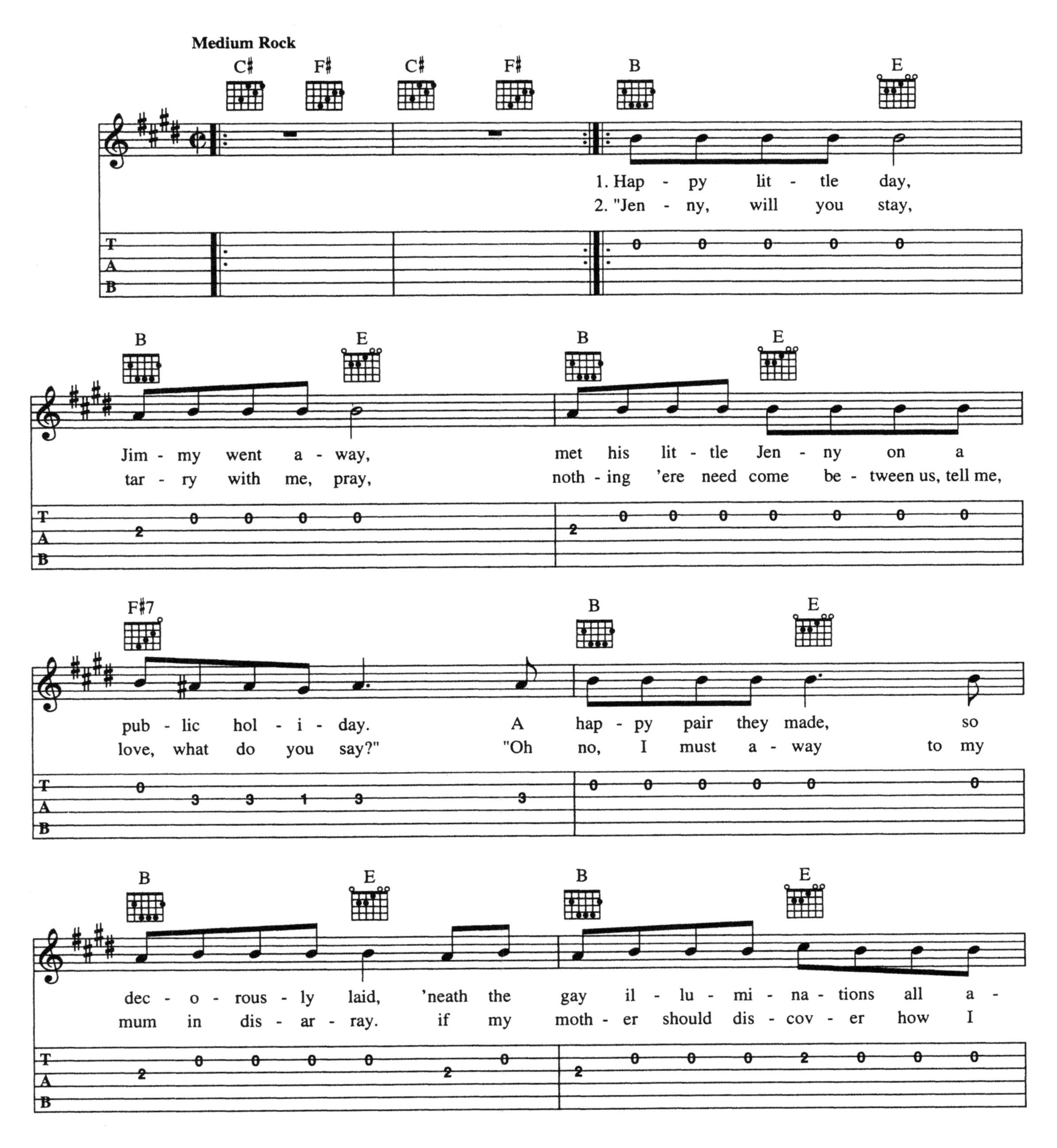

F♯7
A
long the prom - e - nade. It's so good to know there's still a lit - tle
spent my hol - i - day. It would be of small a - vail to talk of
T
A
B

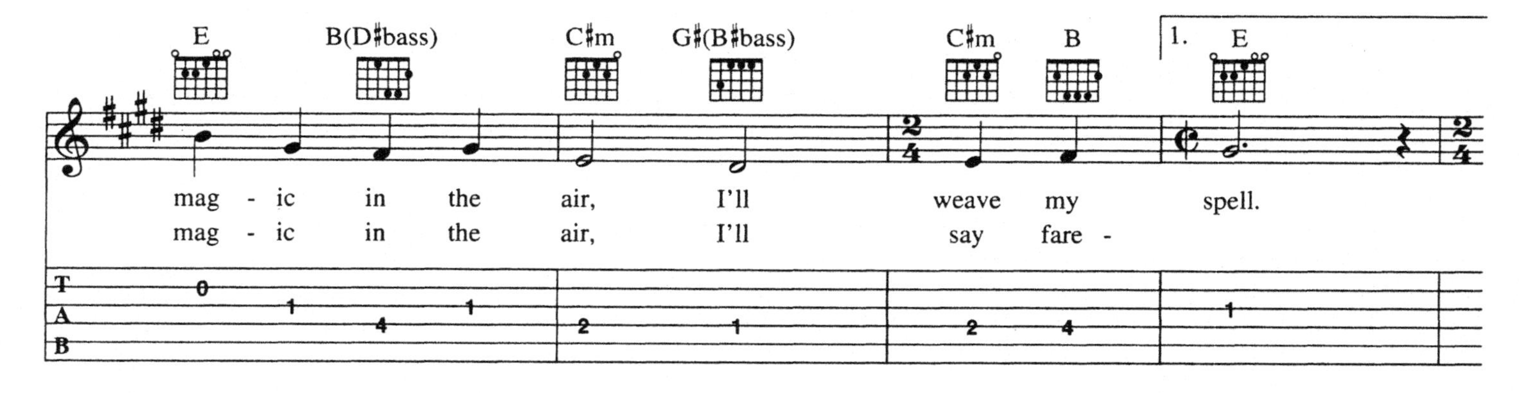
E
B(D♯bass)
C♯m
G♯(B♯bass)
C♯m
B
1. E
mag - ic in the air, I'll weave my spell.
mag - ic in the air, I'll say fare -
T
A
B

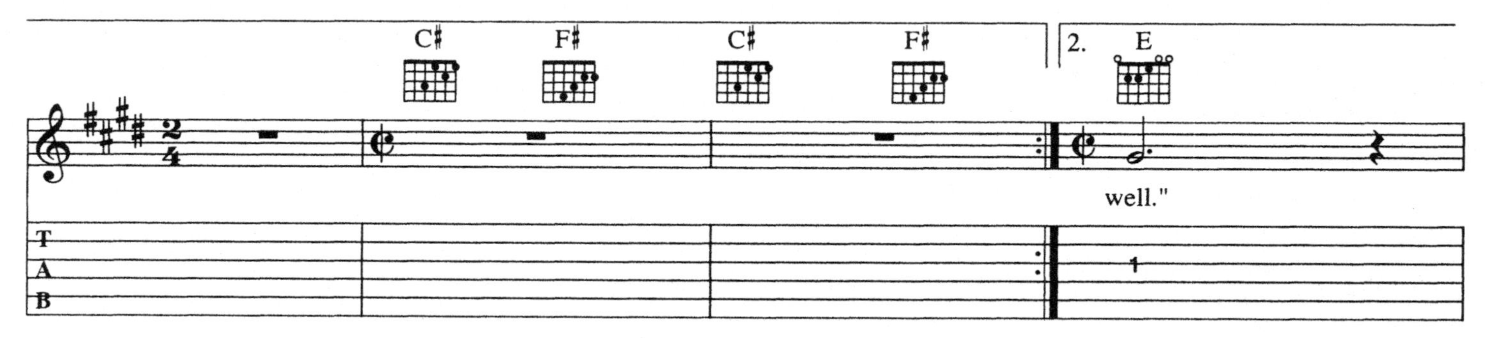
C♯
F♯
C♯
F♯
2. E
well."
T
A
B

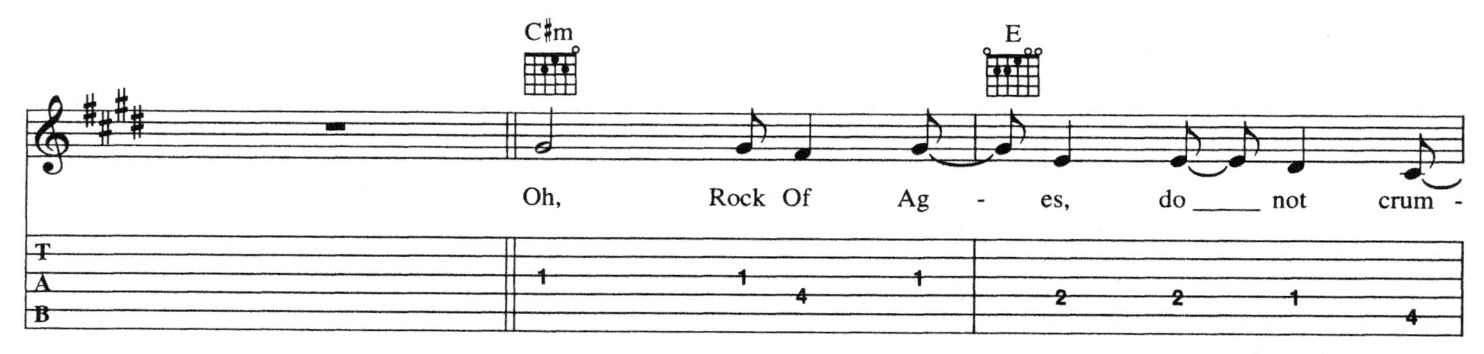
C♯m
E
Oh, Rock Of Ag - es, do not crum -
T
A
B

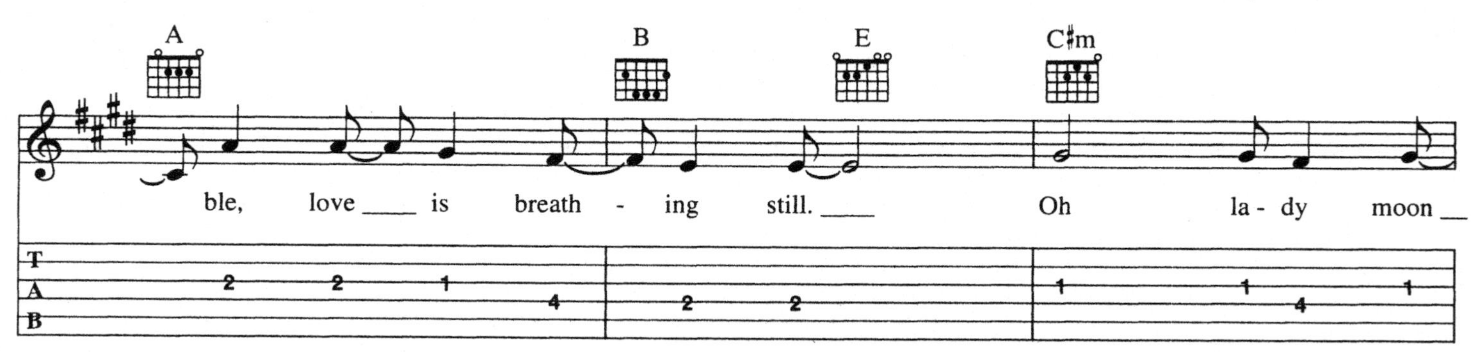
A
B
E
C♯m
ble, love is breath - ing still. Oh la - dy moon
T
A
B

F♯7
B7
___ shine down ___ a lit - tle peo - ple mag - ic if _____ you will. __
A
E
B
E
Jen - ny pines a - way, writes a
B
E
B
E
let - ter ev - 'ry day, "We must ev - er be to - geth - er, noth - ing
F♯7
B
E
can my love e - rase." "Oh no, I'm com - pro - mised, I
B
E
B
E
must a - pol - o - gise, if my la - dy should dis - cov - er how I
F♯7
A
B
E(addG)
spent my hol - i - days."
T
A
B

# FAT BOTTOMED GIRLS

Words and Music by
BRIAN MAY

A
D
life be - fore _ I left my nurs - er - y, left a - lone ___ with big fat Fan - ny, she was
ev - 'ry blue eyed floo - zy on the way. But their beau - ty and their style went kind of
beau - ty queens in this lo - cal - i - ty. Oh, but I _____ still get my plea - sure, still
G
D
A
1.D
such a naugh - ty nan - ny. Heap big wom - an you made a bad boy out of me. ____
smooth af - ter a - while. Take me to them dirt - y la - dies ev - 'ry - time. _
get my great - est trea - sure. Heap big wom - an you gon - na make a big man out of me. __
2. 3.D
Chorus
Hey, hey. __________
2. I've been
Come on.
Now get this
Oh, won't you
Oh, you gon - na
C
G(Bbass)
D
C
A
take me home to - night? __ Oh, down be - side ___ your red fire - light. __
take me home to - night. __ Oh, down be - side ___ your red fire - light. __

D
G
Oh, and you give it all you got, fat bot - tomed girls. _
Oh, you gon - na let it all hang out, fat bot - tomed girls. _
D
A
D
G
You make ___ the rock - in' world __ go 'round. ___ Fat bot - tomed girls _
D
A
To Coda
D
G(Fbass) G(Ebass) D
___ you make __ the rock - in' world __ go 'round.
A
D
G
D
A
D
G
D. S. al Coda
Hey, lis - ten here. ____
3. Now your
Coda
D
Repeat ad lib till fade
'round.
Get on your bikes __ and ride. ____
Fat bot - tomed girls. _

# I WANT TO BREAK FREE

Words and Music by JOHN DEACON

A
To Coda
E
1.
God knows, I want to break __ free.
God knows, I've fal - len in ____ love.
Got to make it on my ___
2. I've fal - len in
T
A
B

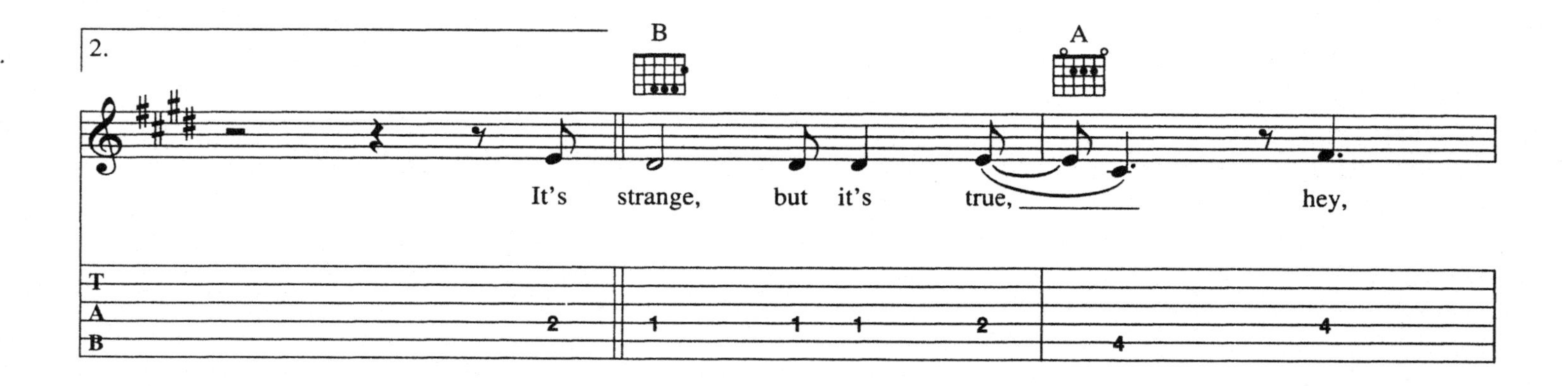
2.
B
A
It's strange, but it's true, ________ hey,
T
A
B

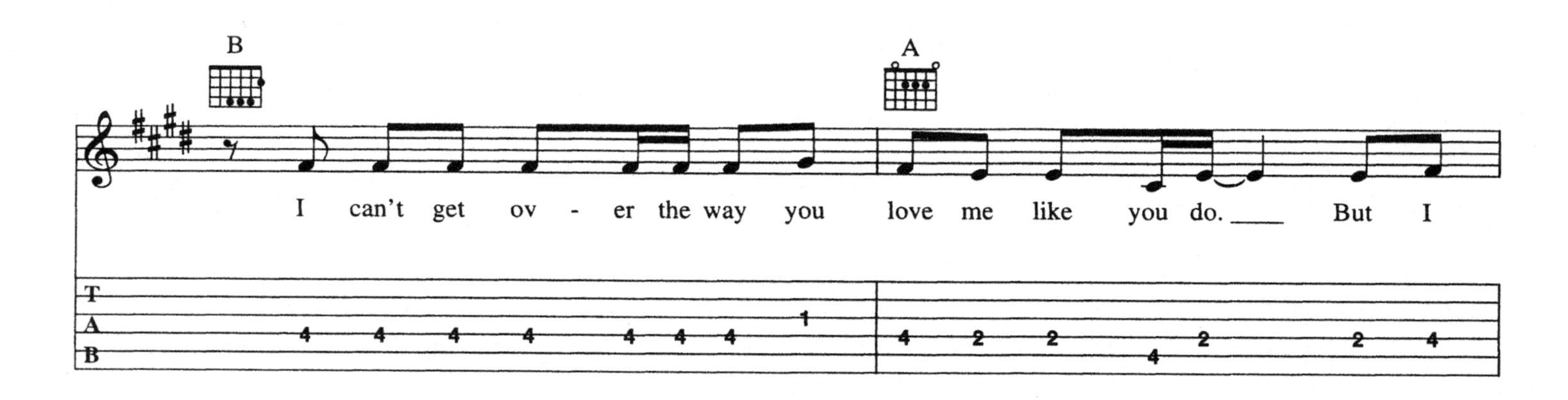
B
A
I can't get ov - er the way you love me like you do. ____ But I
T
A
B

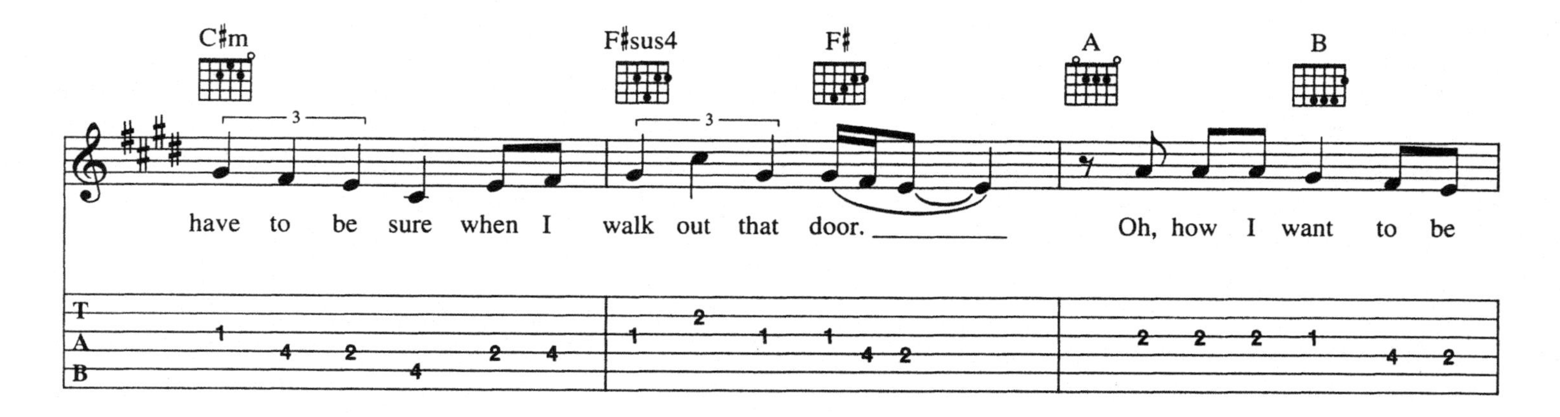
C♯m
F♯sus4
F♯
A
B
have to be sure when I walk out that door. __________ Oh, how I want to be
T
A
B

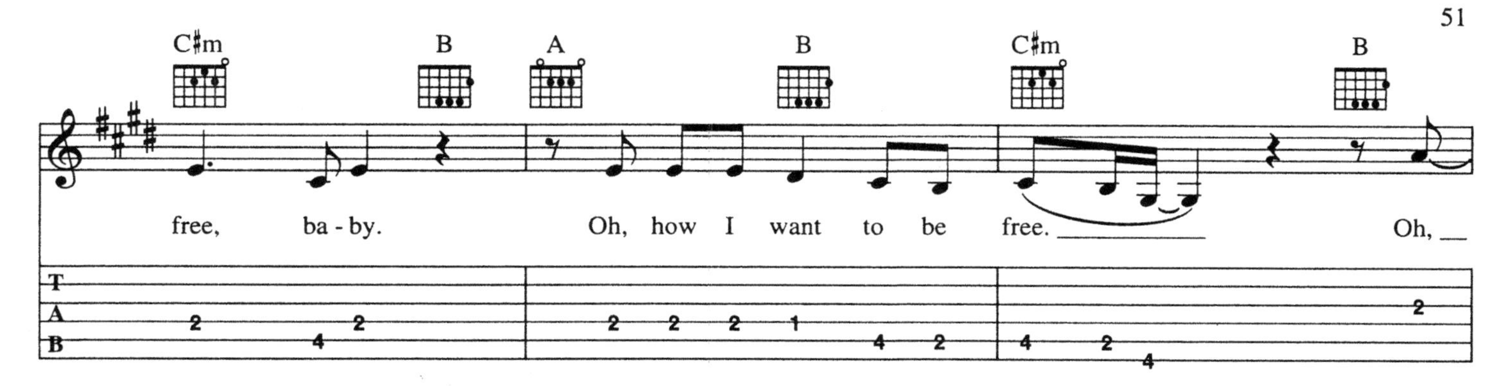
C♯m B A B C♯m B
free, ba - by. Oh, how I want to be free. Oh,

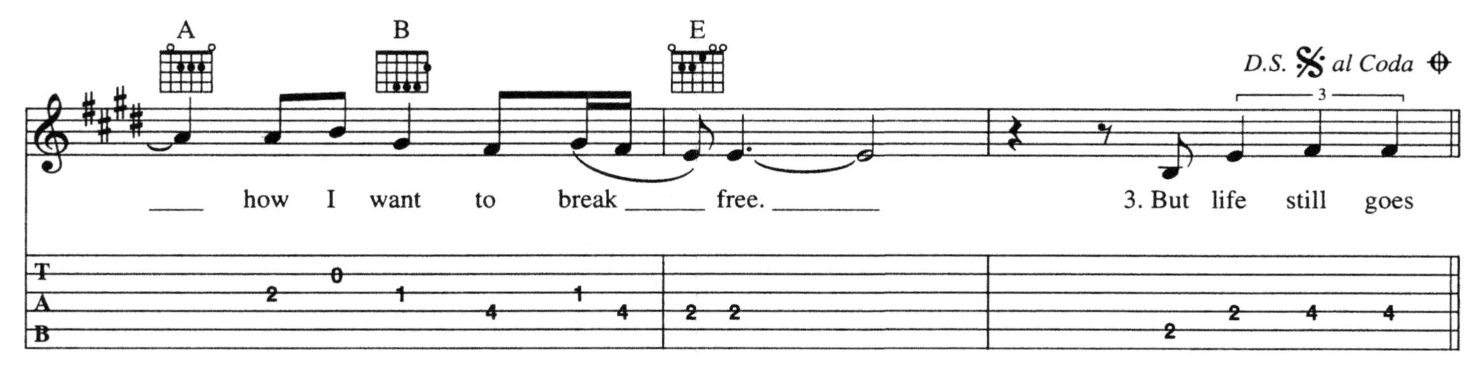
A B E
D.S. al Coda
how I want to break free. 3. But life still goes

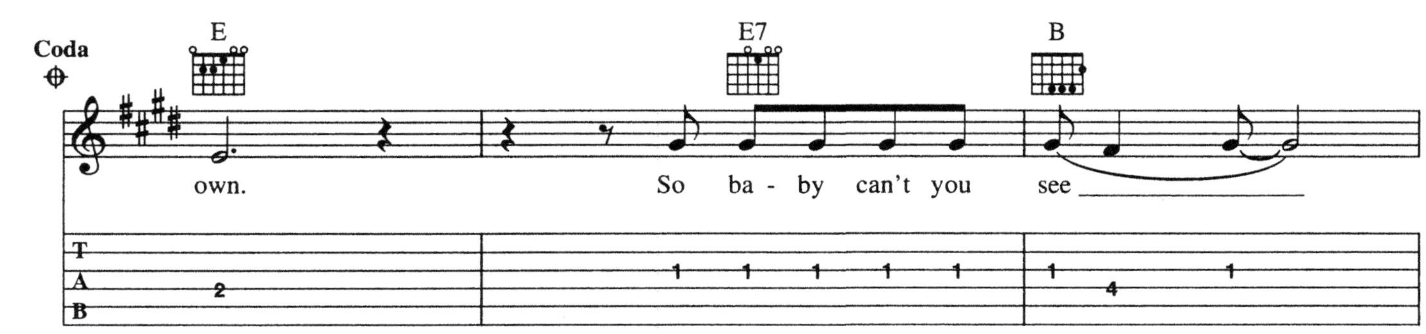
Coda
E E7 B
own. So ba - by can't you see

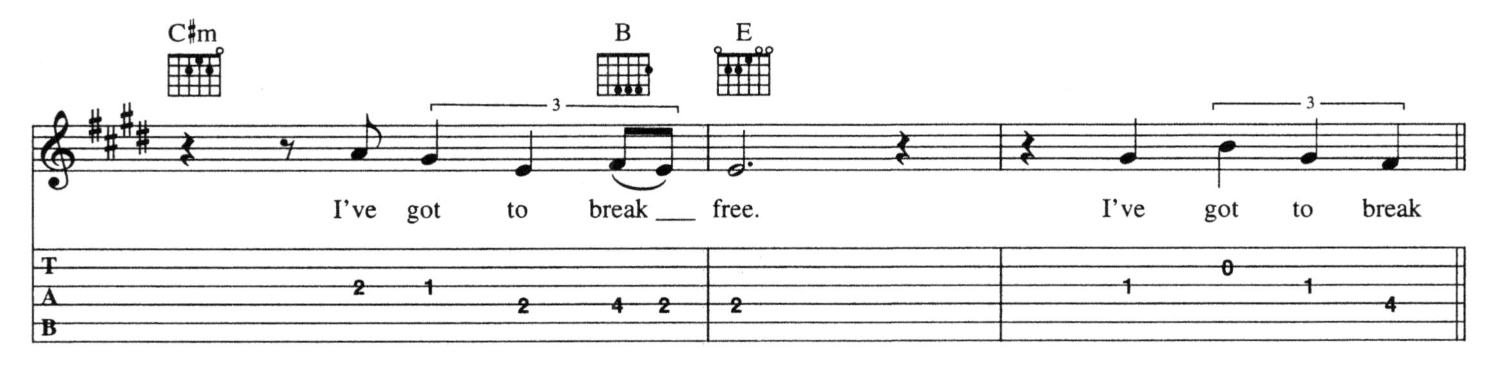
C♯m B E
I've got to break free. I've got to break

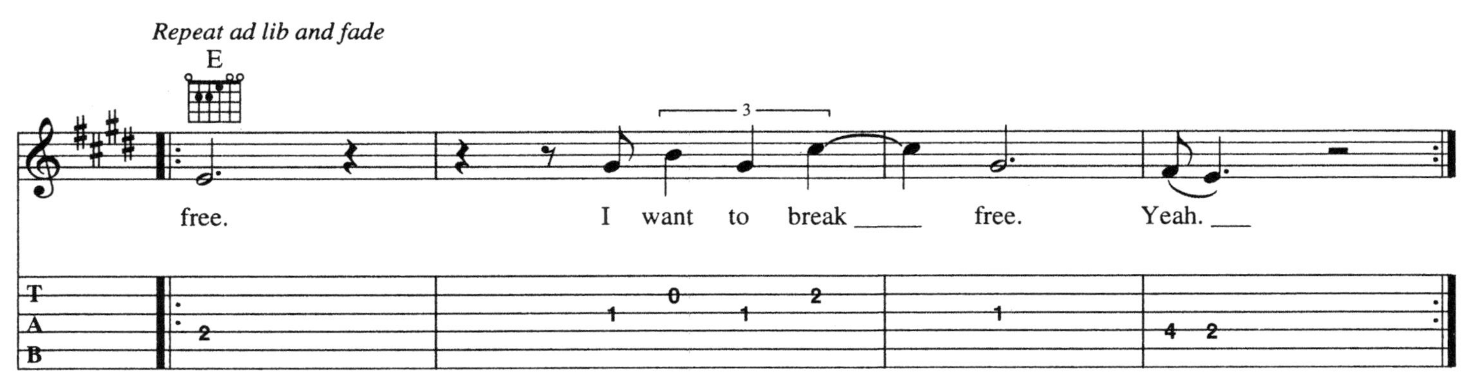
Repeat ad lib and fade
E
free. I want to break free. Yeah.

# KEEP YOURSELF ALIVE

Words and music by
BRIAN MAY

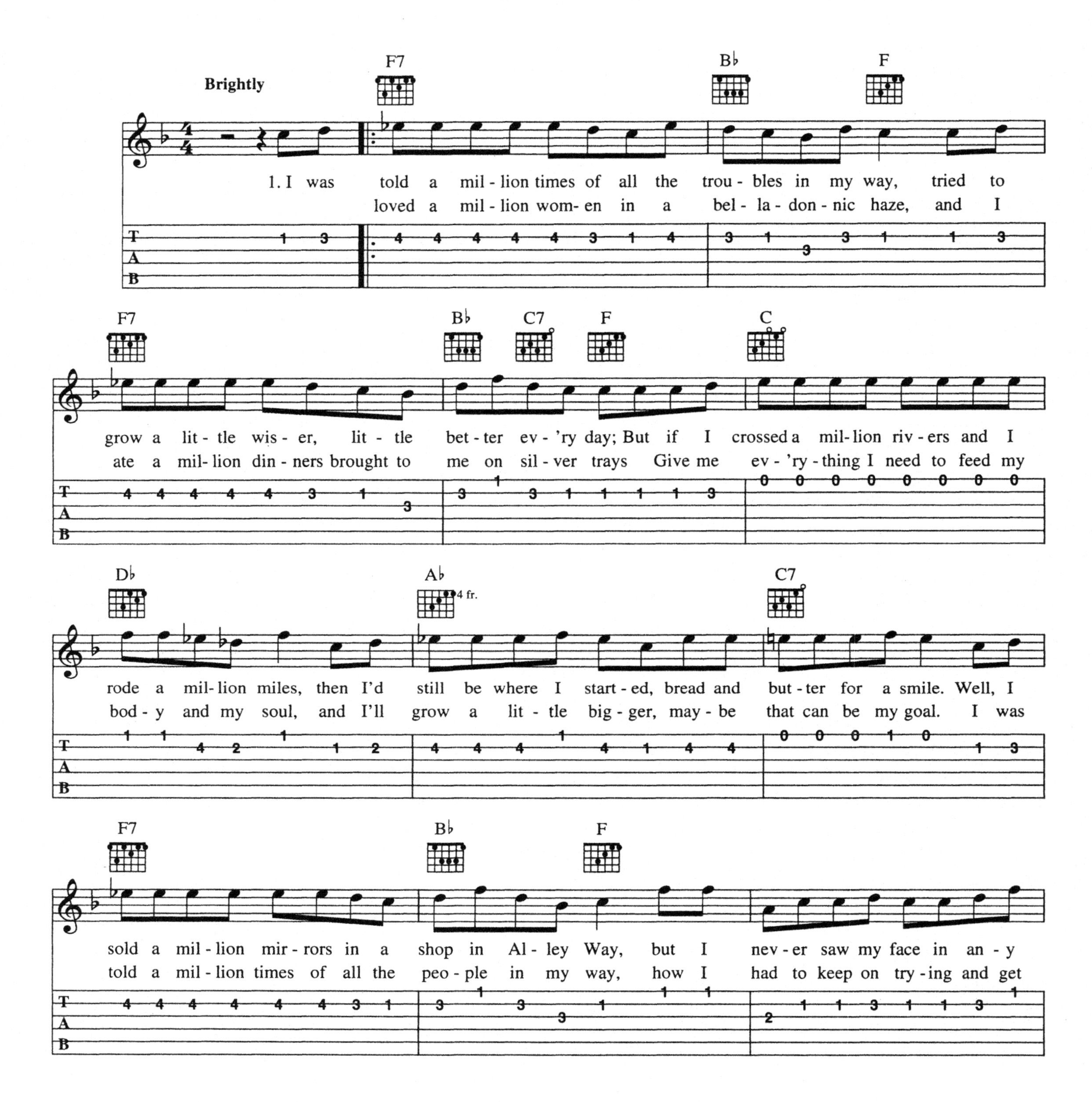

B♭ C7 F C D♭
win - dow an - y day; Well, they say your folks are tell - ing you to be a su - per - star, but I
bet - ter ev - 'ry day; But if I crossed a mil - lion riv - ers and I rode a mil - lion miles, then I'd
A♭ 4 fr. A D G
tell you just be sat - is - fied to stay right where you are.
still be where I start - ed, still be where I start - ed.
Keep your - self a - live,
D. C. 1st time
Segue 2nd time
D A7 D F♯m(C♯bass) Bm G A7 D
keep your - self a - live. It - 'll take you all your time and a - mon - ey, hon - ey, you'll sur - vive.
1.
2.
2. Well, I've
T
A
B

D G D A7 D F♯m(C♯bass) Bm G
Keep your-self a-live, keep your-self a-live. It-'ll take you all your time and a-mon-ey to
C7 F D G D A7
keep your-self a-live. Keep your-self a-live, keep your-self a-live. It-'ll
D F♯m(C♯bass) Bm G A7 D B E
take you all your time and a-mon-ey to keep me sat-is-fied. Keep your-self a-live,
B F♯7 B A♯° G♯m E F♯7 B
4 fr.
keep your-self a-live. All you peo-ple, keep your-self a-live. Take you all your time
and mon-ey, hon-ey, you will sur-vive. Keep your-self a-live, keep your-self a-live.
T
A
B

# PLAY THE GAME

Words and Music by FREDDIE MERCURY

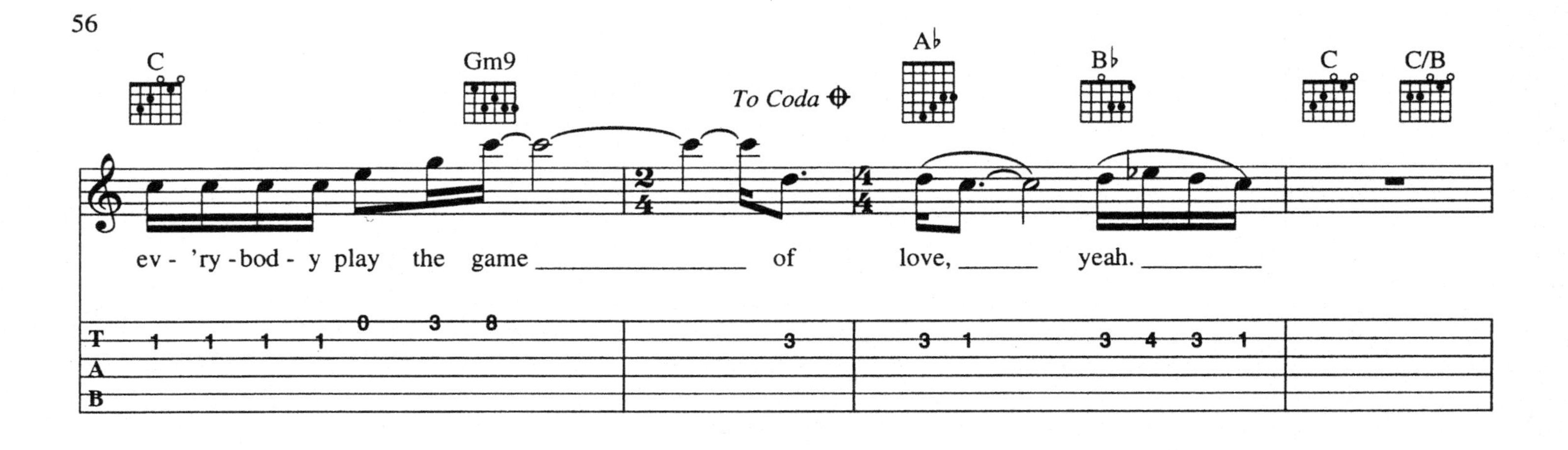
C
Gm9
To Coda
A♭
B♭
C
C/B
ev - 'ry - bod - y play the game of love, yeah.

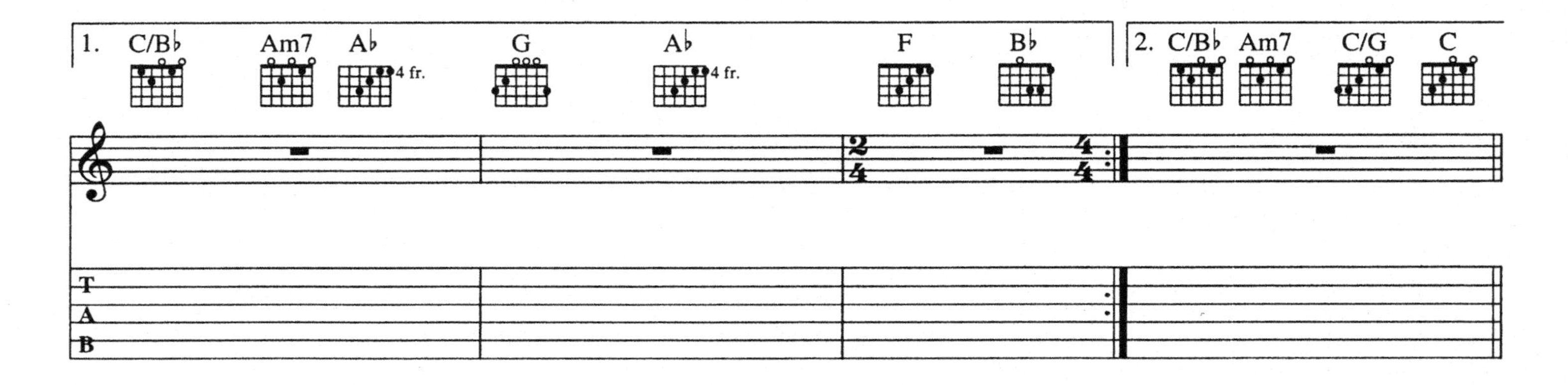
1. C/B♭
Am7
A♭
4 fr.
G
A♭
4 fr.
F
B♭
2. C/B♭
Am7
C/G
C

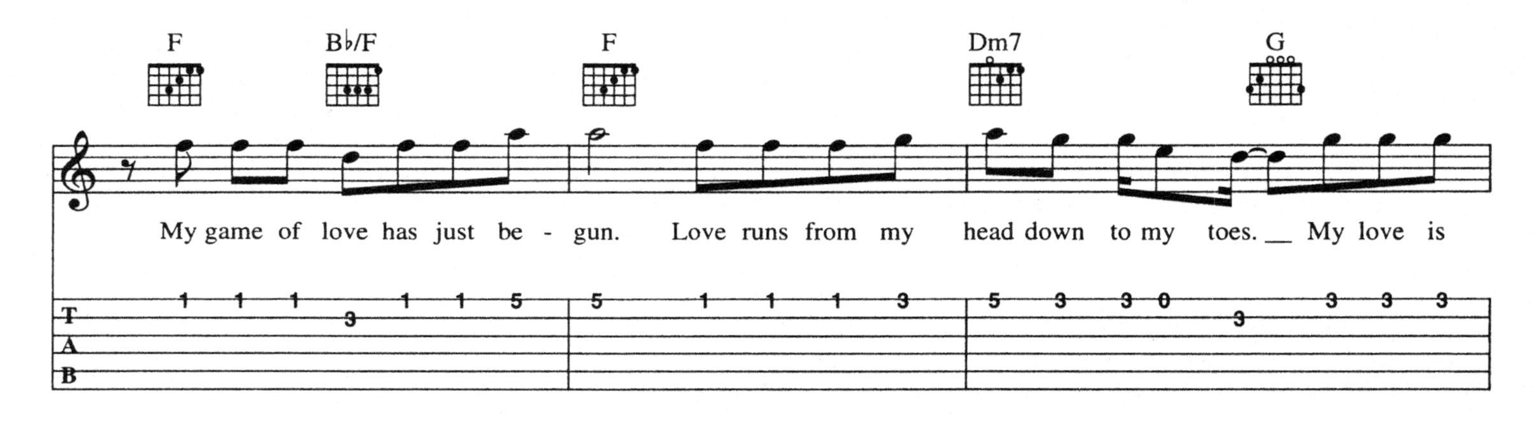
F
B♭/F
F
Dm7
G
My game of love has just be - gun. Love runs from my head down to my toes. My love is

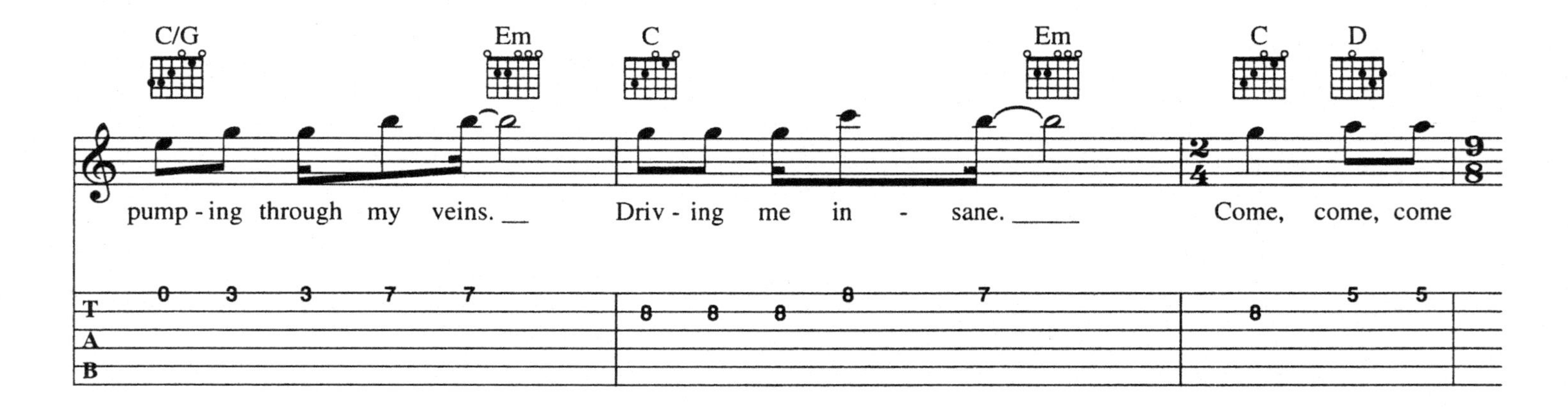
C/G
Em
C
Em
C
D
pump - ing through my veins. Driv - ing me in - sane. Come, come, come

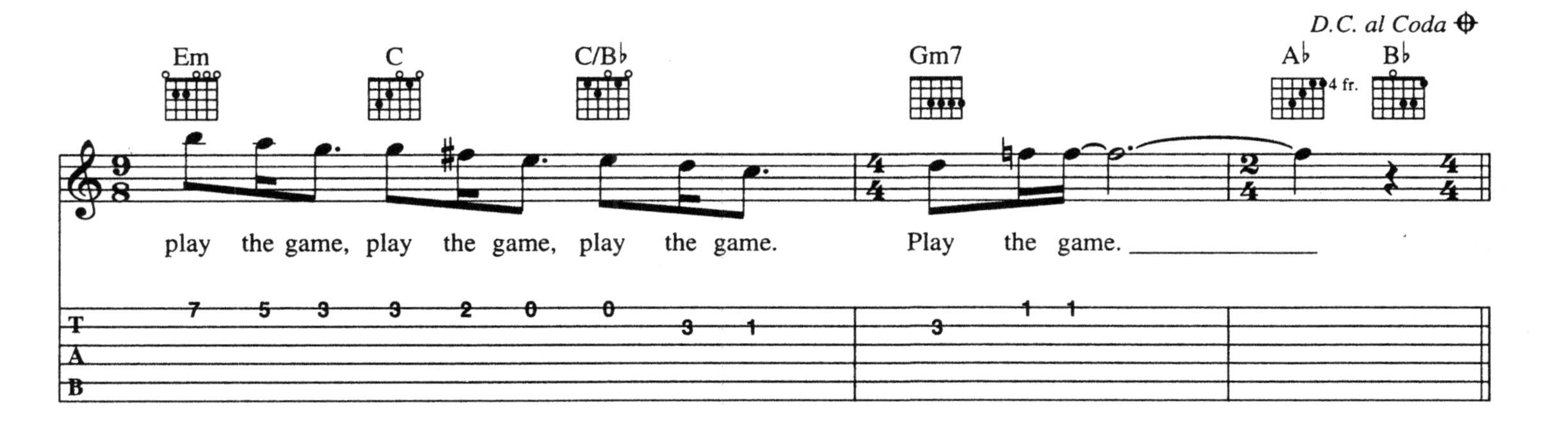
D.C. al Coda
Em
C
C/B♭
Gm7
A♭
4 fr.
B♭
play the game, play the game, play the game.
Play the game.

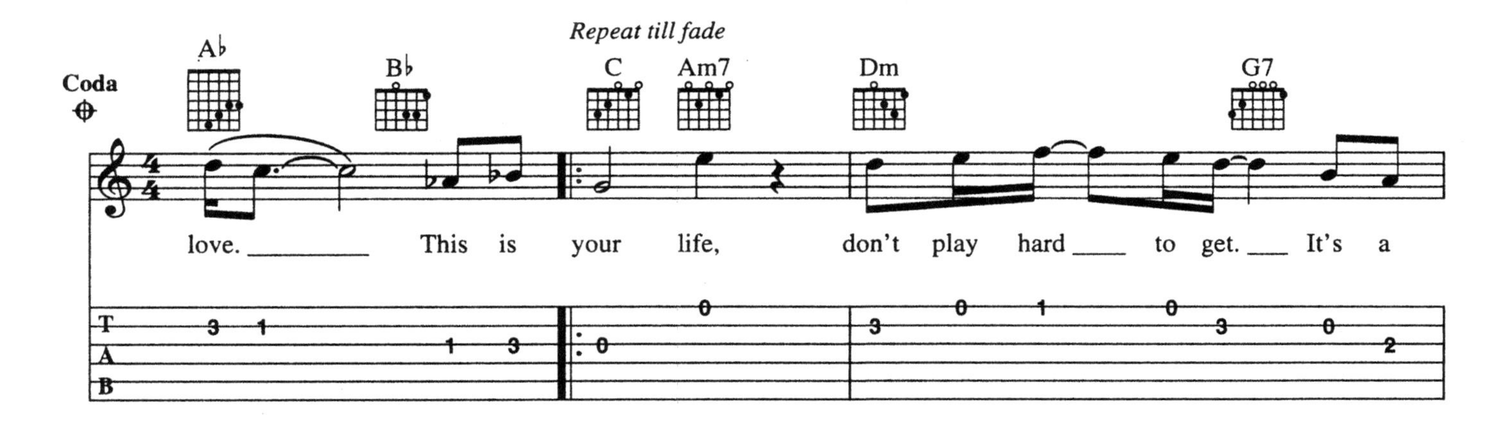
Coda
Repeat till fade
A♭
B♭
C
Am7
Dm
G7
love. This is your life, don't play hard to get. It's a

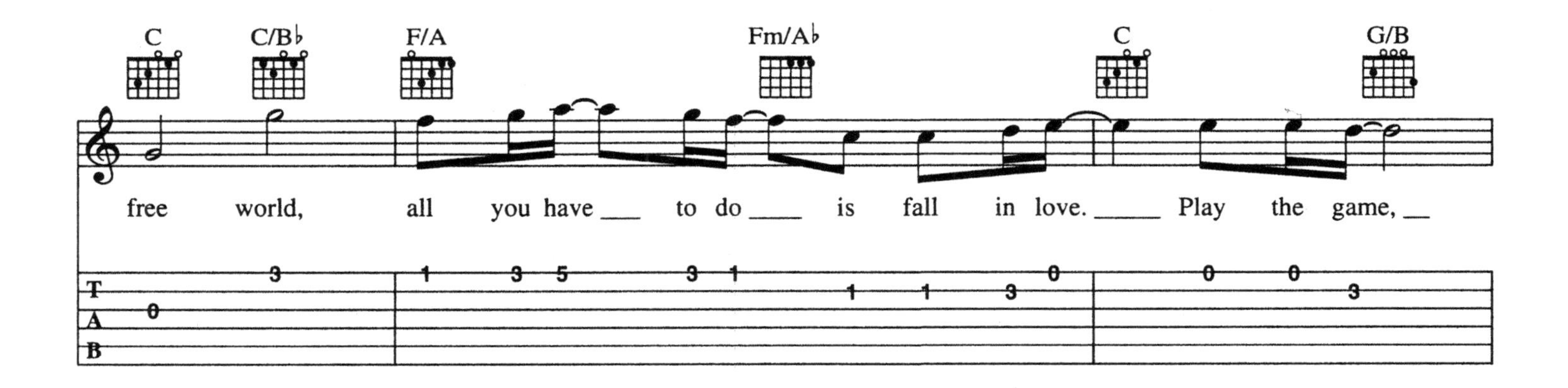
C
C/B♭
F/A
Fm/A♭
C
G/B
free world, all you have to do is fall in love. Play the game,

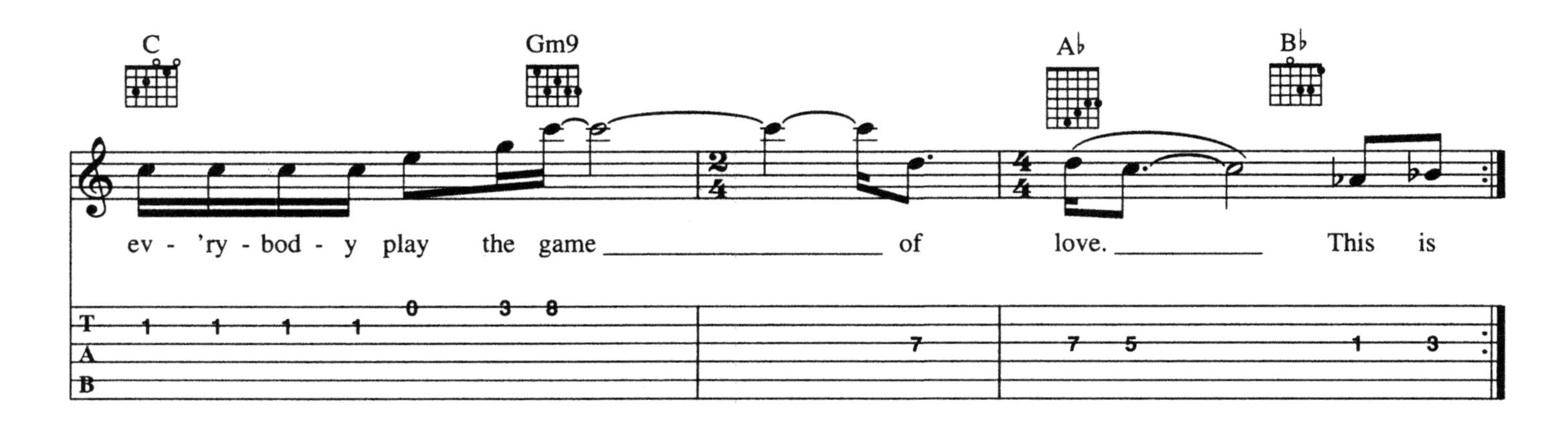
C
Gm9
A♭
B♭
ev - 'ry - bod - y play the game of love. This is

# RADIO GA GA

Words and Music by
ROGER TAYLOR

Fm6/A♭
3 fr.
back - ground noise, __ a back-drop for ____ the girls and boys ____ who
leave, old friend. ___ Like all good things, ____ on you we de - pend. ____ So
B♭
G7/B
just don't know ___ or just don't care, ___ and just com - plain ___ when
stick a - round ___ 'cause we might miss you when we grow tired ___ of
F/C
you're not there. __
all this vis - ual.
You had your time; ___ you had your pow'r. __ You've
C7sus4
C7
B♭
F
Gm/F
F
yet to have ___ your fin - est hour. ___ Ra - di - o.
F/E♭
B♭
F
B♭
F
All we hear ___ is ra - di - o ga ga, ra - di - o goo goo,
T
A
B

B♭
F
F/E♭
B♭
F
ra - di - o ga ga. All we hear ___ is ra - di - o ga ga,
B♭
F
E♭
B♭
To Coda
C
Dm
ra - di - o blah __ blah. Ra - di - o, ____ what's new? __ Ra - di - o, ____
Csus4
C
Csus2
C
F
some - one still loves you.
No Chord
D. S. (no repeats) al Coda
We
Coda
Dm
C
Csus2
C
F
Some - one still loves you.

# TIE YOUR MOTHER DOWN

Words and Music by
BRIAN MAY

G
A
boil - in' up in - side, ain' no way ___ I'm gon - na lose out this time. ___
G
C
A
D
Tie your moth - er down, tie _
A
___ your moth - er down,
lock your daddy out of doors, I don't need him nosin' around.
D
G
D/F♯
tie your moth - er down, tie ___ your moth - er down, give me all your
C
G/B
A
love to - night.

G D/F♯ C G/B A
"You're such a dirt - y louse. Go, get out - ta my house." That's
all I ev - er get from your... your... fam - i - ly ties. In fact,
I don't think I ever heard a single little civil word from those guys!
E
I don't give a light, I'm gon - na make out all right, I've got a
G A
sweet - heart hand to put a stop to all that snipin' an' grousin'.

A G C A D
Tie your moth - er down, tie ___ your moth- er down,
A D
take your little brother swimmin' with a brick, that's all right. Tie your moth - er down, tie _
G D/F♯ C G/B
___ your moth - er down, or you ain't no ___ friend of
A G D/F♯ C G/B
mine. Your

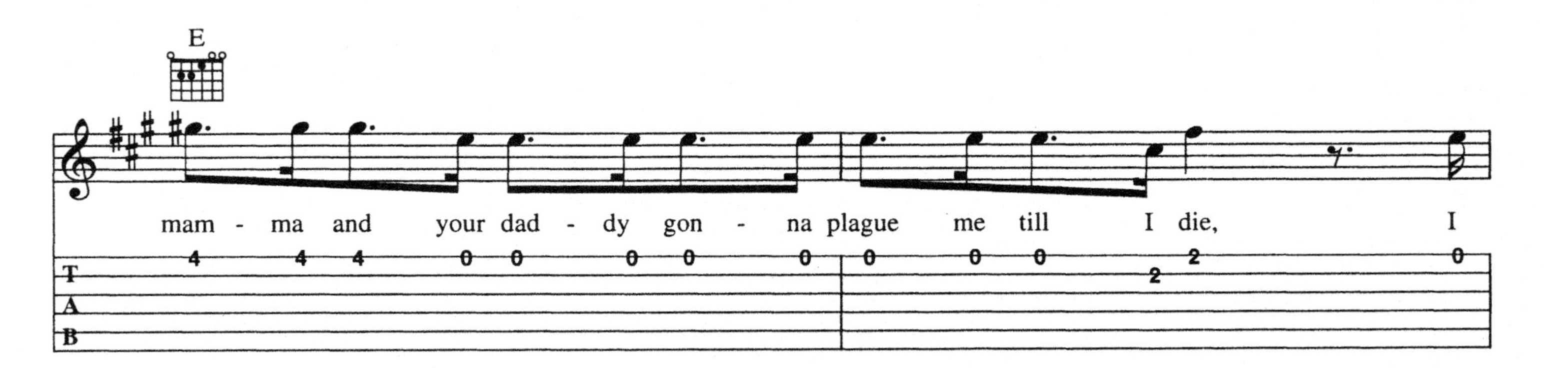
E
mam - ma and your dad - dy gon - na plague me till I die, I

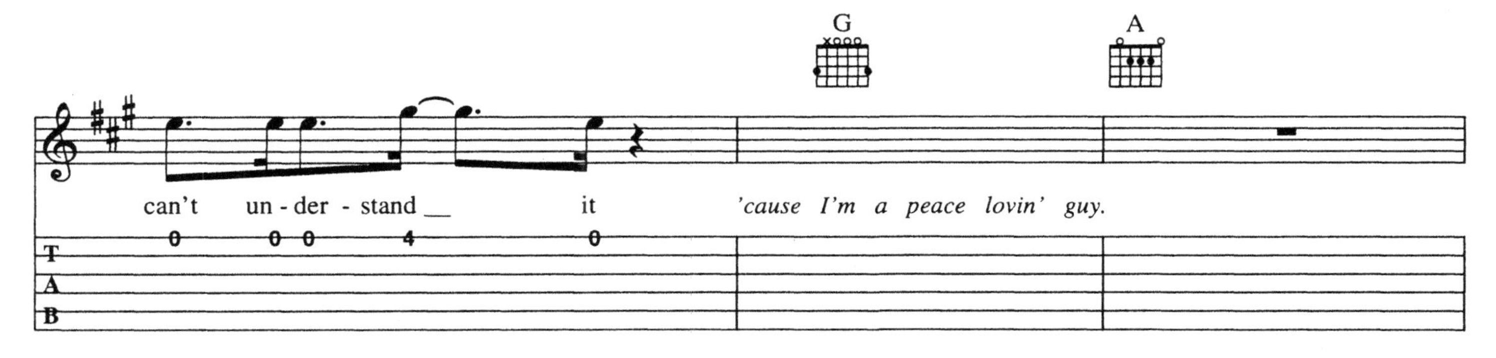
G
A
can't un - der - stand __ it 'cause I'm a peace lovin' guy.
T
A
B

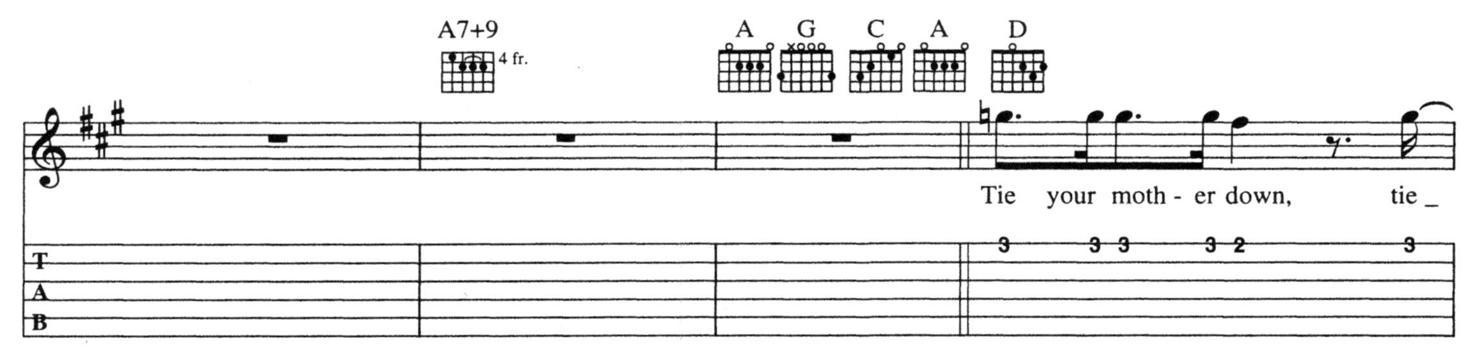
A7+9
4 fr.
A G C A D
Tie your moth - er down, tie _
T
A
B

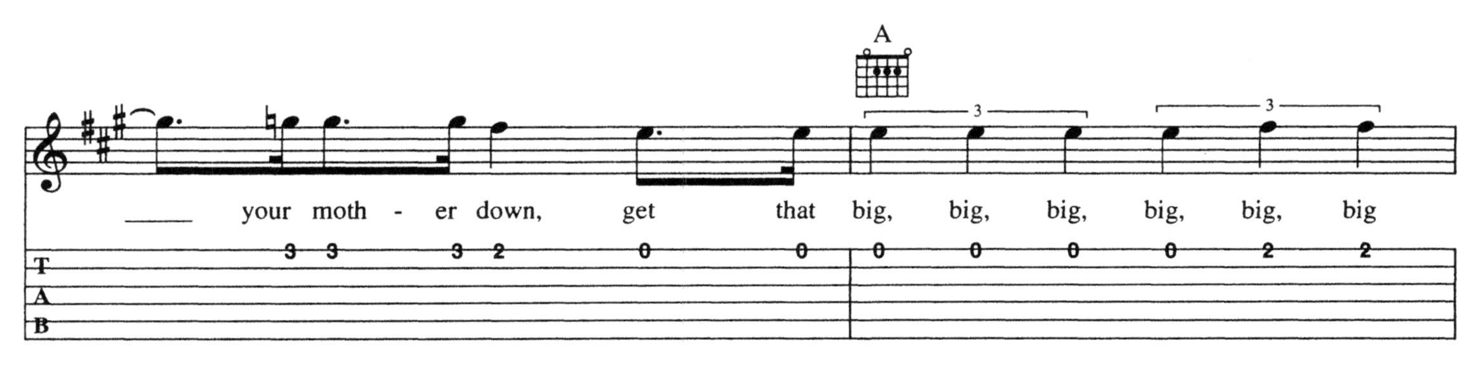
A
_____ your moth - er down, get that big, big, big, big, big, big
T
A
B

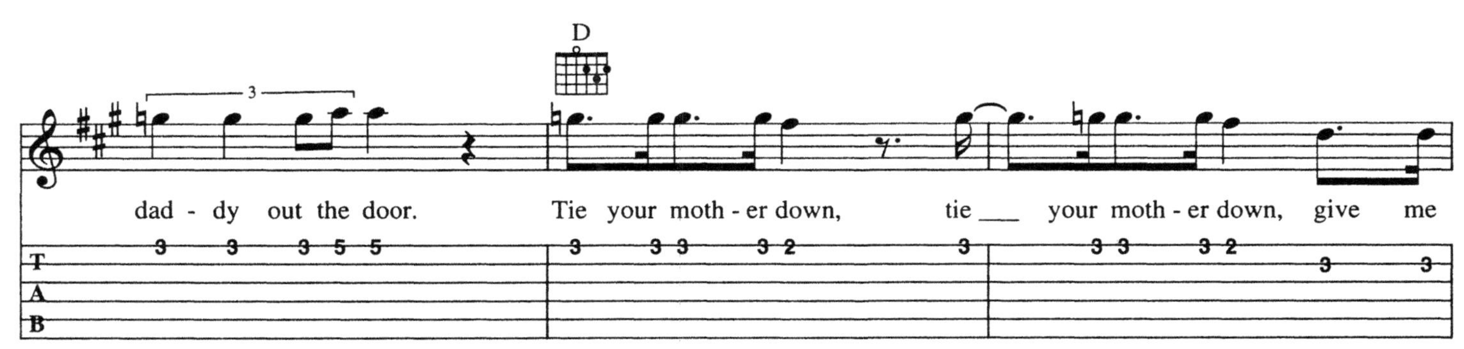
D
dad - dy out the door. Tie your moth - er down, tie ___ your moth - er down, give me
T
A
B

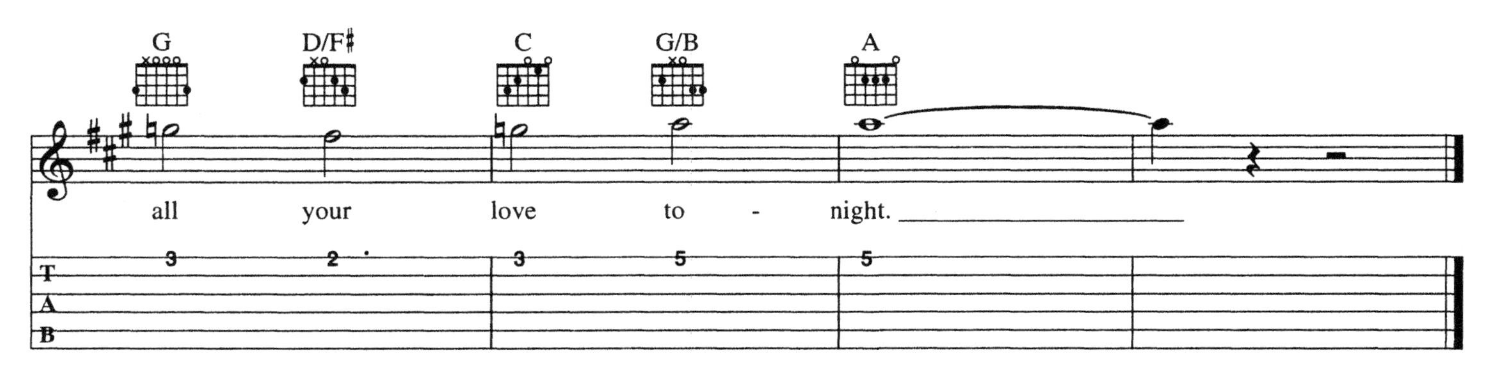
G D/F♯ C G/B A
all your love to - night. ____________________
T
A
B

# WE ARE THE CHAMPIONS

Words and Music by
FREDDIE MERCURY

E♭
B♭(Dbass)
Cm
F7
share of sand ___ kicked in my ___ face but I've come
chal - lenge be - fore the whole hu - man race and I ain't gon - na
B♭
B♭(addC)
C
through.
lose.
And I need to go on, and on, and on, and on.
F
Am7
Dm7
We ___ are the cham - pions ___ my friend. ___
B♭
C
F
Am7
And we'll ___ keep on fight - ing ___ till the
B♭
F♯°
Gm
C(Gbass)
end. ___
We are the cham - pions.

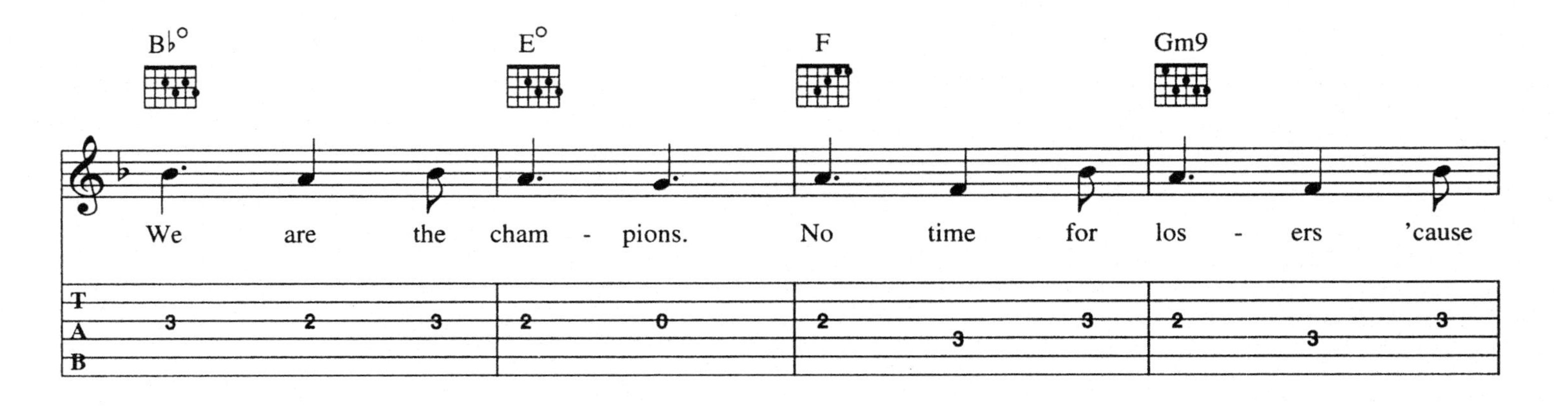
B♭°
E°
F
Gm9
We are the cham - pions. No time for los - ers 'cause
T
A
B

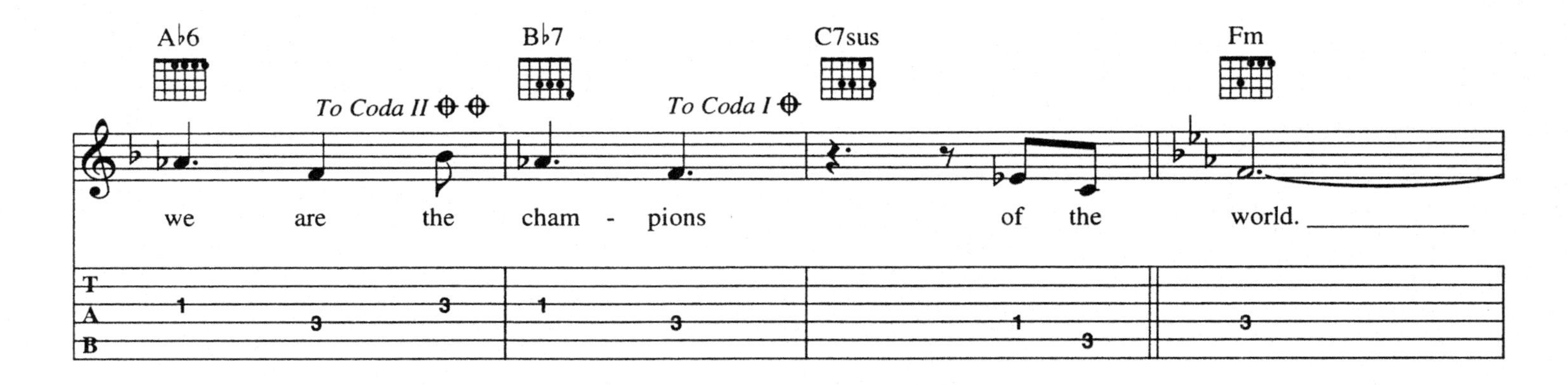
A♭6
B♭7
C7sus
Fm
To Coda II
To Coda I
we are the cham - pions of the world.
T
A
B

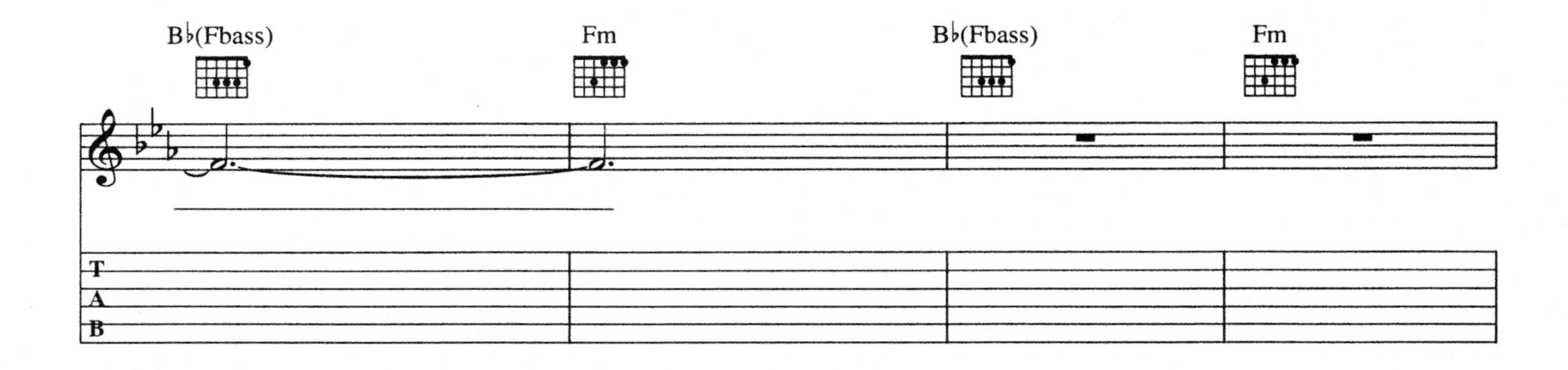
B♭(Fbass)
Fm
B♭(Fbass)
Fm
T
A
B

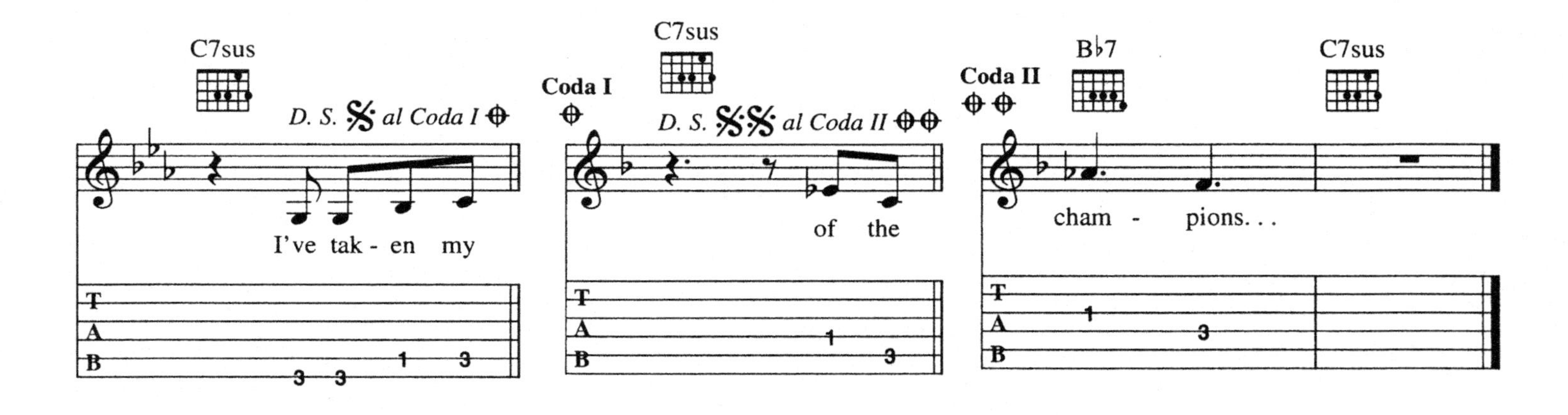
C7sus
D. S. al Coda I
I've tak - en my
Coda I
C7sus
D. S. al Coda II
of the
Coda II
B♭7
C7sus
cham - pions. . .
T
A
B

# WE WILL ROCK YOU

Words and Music by BRIAN MAY

**Moderate**

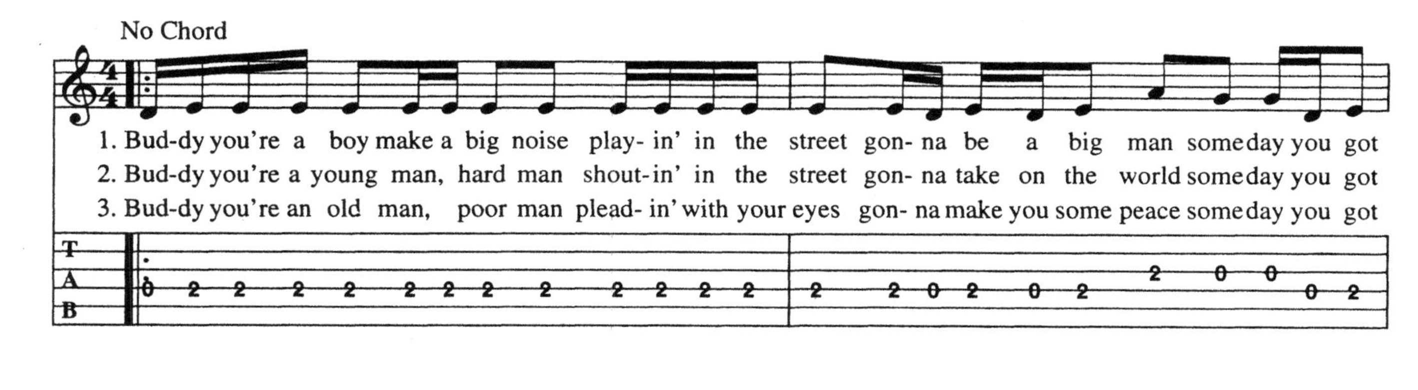
No Chord
1. Bud-dy you're a boy make a big noise play- in' in the street gon- na be a big man someday you got
2. Bud-dy you're a young man, hard man shout-in' in the street gon- na take on the world someday you got
3. Bud-dy you're an old man, poor man plead- in' with your eyes gon- na make you some peace someday you got
T
A
B

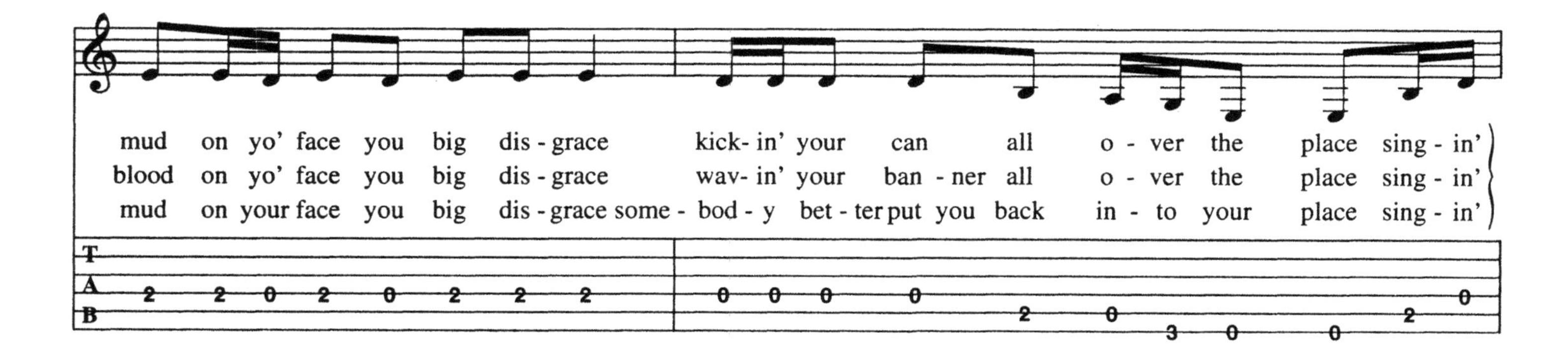
mud on yo' face you big dis - grace kick- in' your can all o - ver the place sing - in'
blood on yo' face you big dis - grace wav- in' your ban - ner all o - ver the place sing - in'
mud on your face you big dis - grace some - bod - y bet - ter put you back in - to your place sing - in'
T
A
B

1.2.
3.
We will we will rock you, we will we will rock you. we will we will
T
A
B

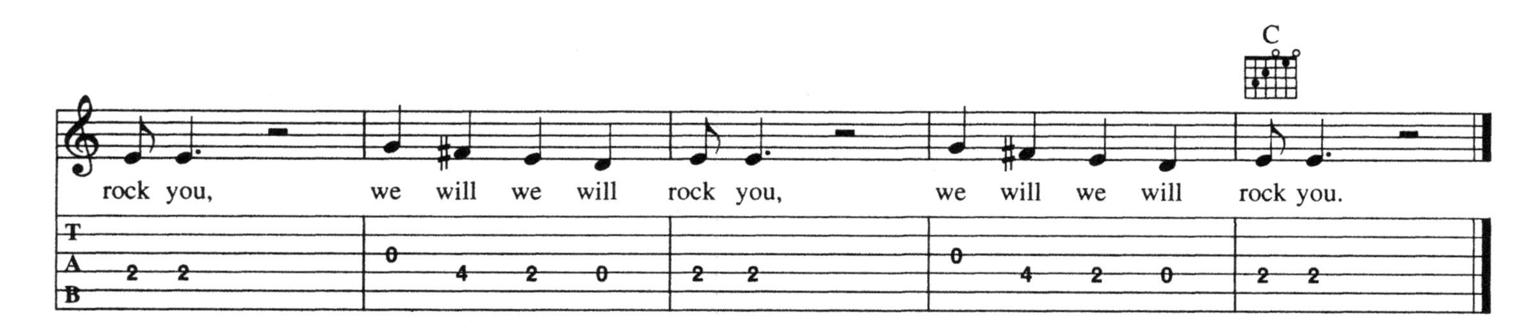
C
rock you, we will we will rock you, we will we will rock you.
T
A
B

# YOU'RE MY BEST FRIEND

Words and Music by
JOHN DEACON

**With a beat**

Dm7(Cbass) C F(Cbass)

1. Ooh, you make me live. ___ What - ev - er this world can
2. Ooh, you make me live. ___ When - ev - er this world is

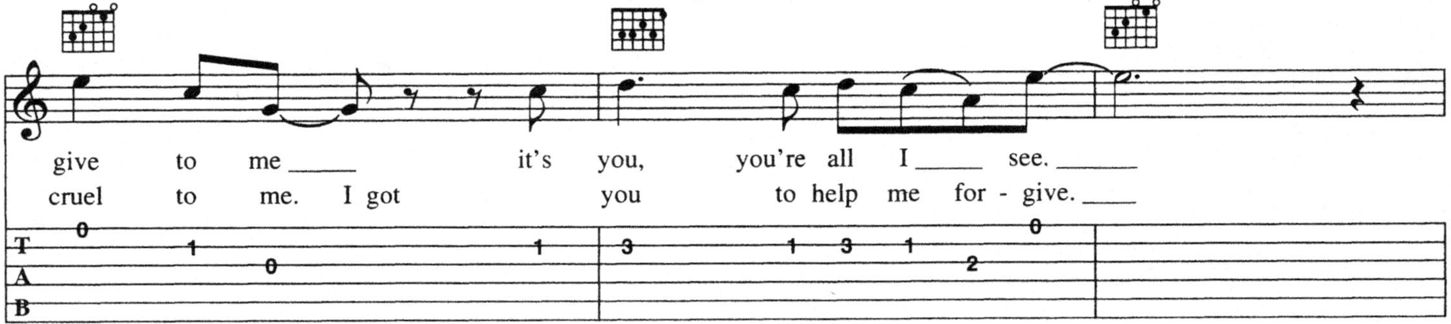
C
Dm7(Cbass)
C
give to me ___ it's you, you're all I ___ see. ___
cruel to me. I got you to help me for - give. ___

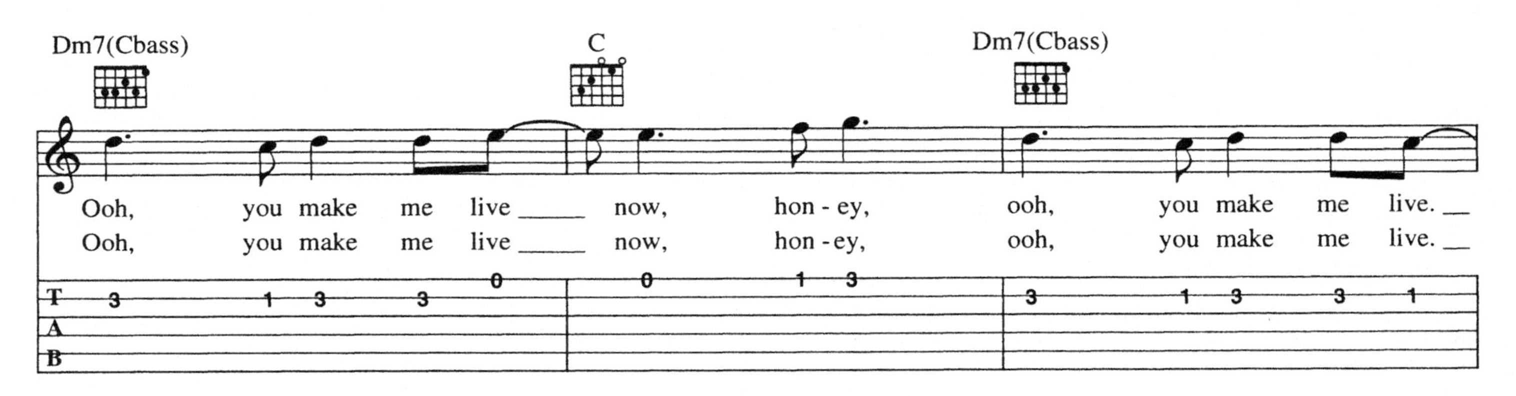
Dm7(Cbass)
C
Dm7(Cbass)
Ooh, you make me live ___ now, hon - ey, ooh, you make me live. __
Ooh, you make me live ___ now, hon - ey, ooh, you make me live. __

C
G
Am
D
F
Ooh, ___ you're the best ___ friend ___ that I ___
Ooh, ___ you're the first ___ one ___ when things __

G7 C G Am D
ever had. I've been with you such a long time. You're my sun-
turn out bad. You know I'll nev-er be lone-ly. You're my on-
F G E Am
shine and I want you to know that my feel-ings are true, I
ly one and I love the things, I real-ly love the
G F Fm C
real-ly love you.
things that you do.
Oh, you're my best friend.
Dm7(Cbass) C E(G♯bass)
Ooh, you make me live. Ooh, I've been
Am C7(B♭bass) F Fm6
wan-der-ing 'round, but I still come back to you. In
T
A
B

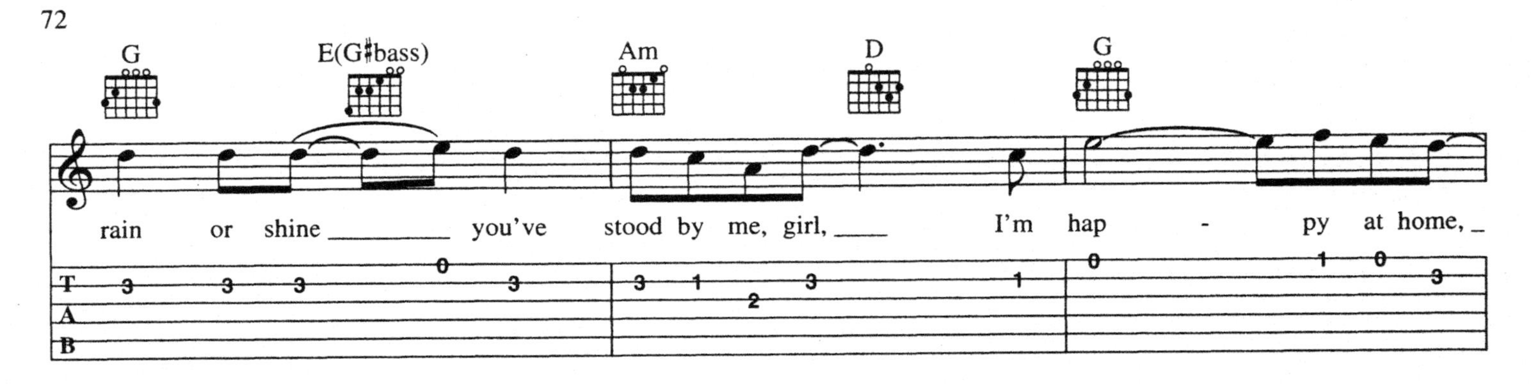
G
E(G♯bass)
Am
D
G
rain or shine ________ you've stood by me, girl, ____ I'm hap - py at home, _

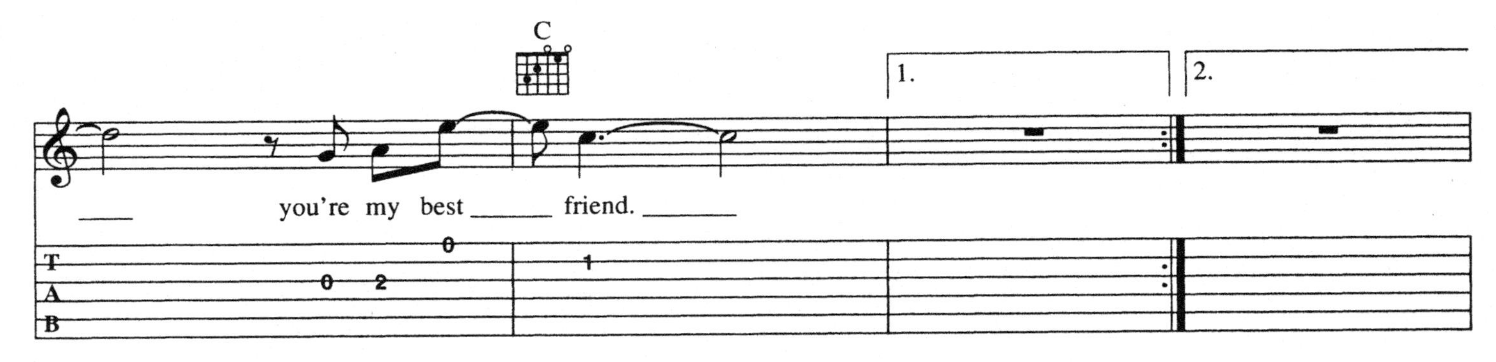
C
1.
2.
____ you're my best _____ friend. _______

Fm6
C
Fm6
C
Ooh, ooh, ____ you're my best ____ friend. _______

Dm7(Cbass)
C
Dm7(Cbass)
C
G
C
Ooh, you make me live, ______ ooh, you're my best friend. ____

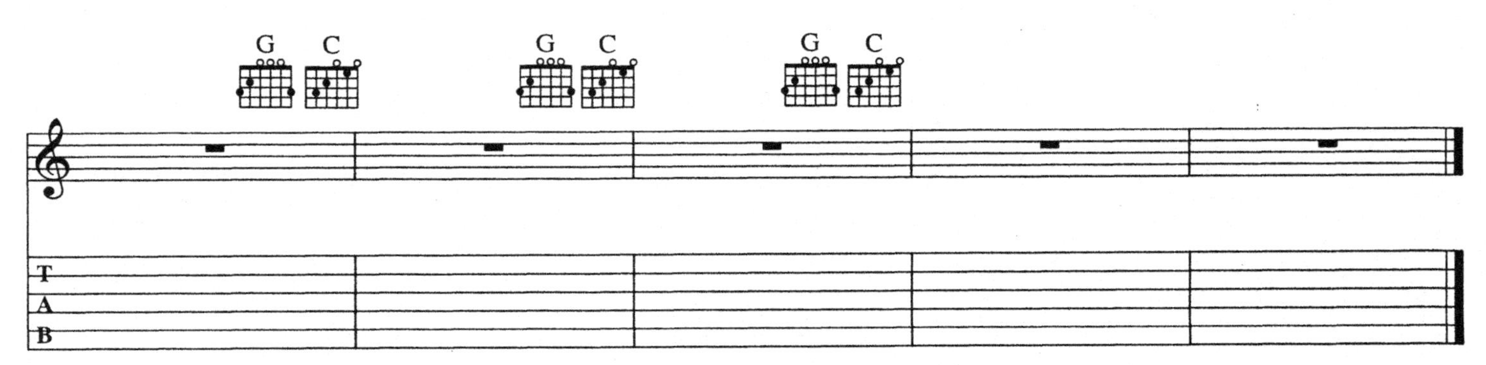
G
C
G
C
G
C